NUMBERS

Books by Jakov Lind

Numbers
Counting My Steps
The Silver Foxes Are Dead and Other Plays
Ergo
Landscape in Concrete
Soul of Wood

NUMBERS

A Further Autobiography

Jakov Lind

1817

HARPER & ROW, PUBLISHERS

New York, Evanston, San Francisco, London

FIRST EDITION

STANDARD BOOK NUMBER: 06–012628–0

LIBRARY OF CONGRESS CATALOG CARD NUMBER: 79–138790

For my
beautiful daughter
Oona

The Lord shall give you meat and you shall eat it.
Not for one day only, not for two days, nor five, nor
ten, nor twenty, but for a whole month you shall eat it
until it comes out at your nostrils and makes you sick;
because you have rejected the Lord who dwells in your
midst, wailing in His presence and saying: "Why did we
ever come out of Egypt?"

NUMBERS 11:18–20

Concerning the immediate objects in illusions,
hallucinations, and dreams it is meaningless to ask
whether they "exist" or are "real." Because they are
and that ends the matter.

Bertrand Russell, *Mysticism and Logic*

Though born in the Danube valley, I feel actually more at home at high altitudes. Thin air is my element; the higher up, the thinner the air, the more I gasp for it, the more I experience my true background. My paternal ancestors lived in the Tatra mountains. My origin is high, in the head. Whether the fathers of my fathers believed in a primary cause I can't tell (my father never discussed it with me), but they left me all the same with this head I now begin to see in close-up. It all begins high in the head, with or without oxygen.

In Genesis it says: בראשית *(Hebrew for "In the beginning"). It didn't start in history and therefore not with my father nor with his, but* IN THE BEGINNING GOD CREATED HEAVEN AND EARTH. *(The Hebrew word* rosh, *meaning "head," is in this* בראשית*). If Genesis were wrong in this assumption, I might have felt it somewhere else first—in my nose maybe, or in the eyes, the ears, the mouth—yet it's nowhere but in the head. Here is the beginning. In this head there is a God that created heaven and earth;*

you don't have to believe it, but if you do it makes sense. God didn't create anything in the middle or the end—everything in its beginning. That God and not I myself created this is very likely. I was caused by my father and he by his father and so on ad infinitum back to Adam, back to the primordial Adam, and right back into the beginning where God, before He made man, long before him, created first a heaven to look at and an earth for us to stand on. No problems so far. Here is my face. Nose, eyes, ears, mouth, hair, cheeks, et cetera. The problem begins when I wonder where all this is going and what all this means. The fact that I see my face (recognition) leads to other trails of thought spiraling up in smoke, dancing as tiny colored rings in front of half-closed eyes. There I am, mystery and all; I look at myself and begin to presume that there is a difference between my face and other faces, a difference between man and man, man and animal, animal and plant, et cetera: in close-up I see difference and not sameness. I see uniqueness in creation and not a heap of mud. Where is the problem? It's coming. Once I see this uniqueness in my face (just by looking at it, an experience too common to be generally noticed) and a uniqueness in everything, I perceive the idea of a material I cannot see (soul or spirit) that must have been before I could see the face. Let me try to describe it in numerical order.

1. The beginning
2. Distinction between one thing and another
3. Idea, which makes me also recognize the specific of the self
4. The presumption that there must be a container to con-

tain the self, but this container, the soul, cannot be visualized nor can it be imagined

5. The content of this container, the body, leaves the container or is left by it, at some stage of union.

6. Knowing this to be true, it follows I want paradise now rather than later, as the present fusion, which results in consciousness, seems adequate. You know what you have, but hardly what you will get in the next world.

7. Therefore life may seem to be hell compared to the paradise it could be if I did not know of it.

8. What Freud termed death instinct, the libido, is hard to gratify. When you are dead you cannot enjoy the knowledge of good and evil either. Why presume it should be easier now? The Fall is the best thing that could have happened.

9. Because without this knowledge of good and evil there would have been no need for God.

10. Yet God is not primarily a moral issue but a way of looking at things, at the totality of His creation.

Considering the state of the ecology, the population that grows and keeps on growing, considering the arsenal of Hitlers—all marked H—buried underground, which may be let loose one day if we don't remember this very uniqueness, I am an optimist. Optimism is something I learned in several stages and in many strange and peculiar ways.

J. L.

New York
February, 1972

PART ONE

When I came back to the familiar smells and noises, I was ready to stay at the docks and ask for a job as a porter. I was in love with Marseilles and thought it the most beautiful town in the world. Its wharves and warehouses, boulevards, parks, narrow alleys and steep stairs wind up to a white church high above the town, while the town itself is a landscape of sunshine and blue seas. Finally a real town and I am finally back in a real world. No more "Next year in Jerusalem" for me. I was back in my old sick skin of "ordinary human being." There was a time when I thought there is no escape, no way out, no future and no expectation. There was a time when I thought that whatever has to happen in this world, it has to happen now. In 1950 a hammer promised work and a sickle a harvest of plenty; it said so on the billboards. Everyone who votes for Thorez, it said, will have his share. It is either changing the world with the help of Lenin or Stalin, or praying for a better life. There was nothing else one could do here in Europe. In Israel there had been no need to pray, but here a "change of world" takes place around the clock.

3

I was going back to where I wanted to go back with a mystical thirty-five dollars in my pocket. Not enough to make it from Vienna to Amsterdam. Should Honig disappear with the hundred and fifty dollars we were supposed to pick up in Vienna, it looked like the end of everything. No Amsterdam equaled no divorce equaled no new life. Brösel convinced me that Abraham, when he left Ur in Chaldea, had even less. Just twenty-two letters and ten numbers, according to the cabalists, "and look what he made of it! Your private finances are unimportant. What matters: Do you know where you are going?"

Know where you are going? Who knows such things? I didn't know where I was going, not exactly, and wasn't going anywhere in particular. I just *was*. I existed—I suffered. I only saw circles inside circles, one inside the other, but no more. Now, a little higher up the tree of life, I can see a bit more of the light into which all of it will ultimately disappear. If my eyes had opened up at twenty-three, I might have been blinded by all this light. Existence equaled a mixture of sadness, qualms, doubts and self-pity. Sorry for Ida, for myself, for my sisters I'd left behind. I felt sorry. My only hope was in a future that looked even grimmer. "Israel left Egypt as the soul leaves the body to unite with its maker," Brösel claimed, but not me. I left Israel so I could wait somewhere else for the day of redemption. For me the tragicomedy called "Jew" was over and finished once and for all, I was mad enough to believe. I will be a cosmopolitan, citizen of the world, and that's all. That citizen of the world, cosmopolitan and Jew are more or less the same thing didn't occur to me then.

All I really wanted was to see the old chestnut trees, gray skies, big, dark buildings, real green grass for a change. I was sick of blue skies. I had seen enough unemployment and bad times. I was an idealist no longer. The fleshpots of Egypt smelled of something new and exciting.

"What are you? A crazy existentialist?"

"What's an existentialist? I'm an actor." My passport said *Actor*.

"Where do you act?"

"I'll find out. Sooner or later."

"Try to get into metals and minerals; you'll do better. If you can't get into steel or iron, try to get into natural gas, oil or coal. But of course if you can get into diamonds, gold, silver or any other precious stone you are even smarter."

"Why be smart?"

"Look at it like this: the world is full of treasures, right? All one has to do is find them, dig them up and sell them. What more do you need in life?"

Fritz Brösel was off to Canada to study mining. He was about my age, twenty-three, had a straight, thin nose and beautiful white teeth and was a bachelor. Maybe he did know better. The Brösels always know everything; the cynics always seem more clever than I, with my vague creative ideas. Compared to Fritz Brösel, who shared with Ida a "normal" outlook on what life is supposed to be all about (looking after oneself), I was a child. He irritated me. I hated him. I didn't like his speeches. I envied him his beautiful white teeth, straight, thin nose (mine is straight but not thin) and his uncle Herbert Broslinsky, who went to Montreal in '38, started with nothing, and could now afford to pay the school fees so his nephew could learn the art of getting at metals and minerals. Brösel saw I envied him for his excursion to the New World (that's what we still called the U.S. in '50) and assured me that I too could make it in Canada or the U.S. "All you need is to make money; the rest is easy. If you are rich, people think you are the greatest actor in the world. In fact you *are* the greatest actor if you can pull it off."

The idea of making money disgusted me. "What's money? Money is there to be spent; it's shit. Nothing. *Merde*."

"Like hell. With money you can buy the most beautiful women and the most brilliant brains. What more do you want?"

"I know there is something else, but I can't think of it right now."

"What do you see when you close your eyes?"

"Circles inside circles, one inside the other."

"You are definitely wasting your time. You should see gold rings and jewelry, not circles. You must be an existentialist."

I hadn't given it much thought. Existentialism was something people talked about. It was the fashion to wear black berets, corduroy trousers and black shirts and to talk about existentialism. "No, I'm not an existentialist. I don't even know what it is."

"What do you think about the human condition?"

"The communists will take over one day."

"Nonsense. The Jews will take over the world. Without the Jews at the helm, the masses might destroy the world."

"Central committees are there to keep the masses under control."

It was a difficult and dangerous crossing. The sea was rough and the sky all shades of gray. On the second day people

6

unpacked their "European" garments and looked fatter, paler and more worried. Most of the other eight hundred passengers didn't know what was waiting for them ashore either. I was not part of these people; I was a special case. An actor in search of a good play he might have to write himself. I didn't like the word *artist* and I didn't like to be counted among the existentialists. An existentialist was anyone who could not make ends meet, couldn't look after his own affairs, and therefore discussed "the human condition."

My concern was for "humans," not "humanism"; individuals, not movements. All the same, I believed that communism must ultimately conquer the world, not because I liked the idea but because the majority of the people of this world seemed to or were forced to like it that way, which comes down to the same thing. Brösel hated "the people." I only felt a stranger among them. He tried to convince me that "the people," "the masses," are out to destroy the world and have therefore to be controlled. He wanted to convince me that only God, with the help of His chosen people, could cope with a strong, universal desire for self-destruction. I believed neither in Brösel's God nor in Brösel's Jews.

"Why do you hate 'the people,' Fritz?"

"Who says I hate them? I love them. They are beautiful. All of them. All people are blessed by Him up there to grow up, be happy and live in peace forever after, amen, my father said—but what happens?"

"I don't know. What happens?"

"They can't."

"Why not?"

"Because they don't know how to."

"Why not?"

7

"Because no one tells them."

"Why do those who know how to live well not tell those who don't know?"

"It's not like that."

"How is it?"

"It's like this. Among those who know, some tell and some don't. Among those who tell, some tell it wrong and some too loud. And among those who tell it right, some set an example to help others and others don't. They are the arrogant rabbis. We know them all. So who is left to tell the people?" He stared at me.

"Who?"

"The saints. And how many saints are there? How many saints are there in the world? Come on, think!"

"A few."

"Well, those few tell everyone how to live, but what happens?"

"What happens?"

"You tell me."

"I don't know."

"They tell them and the people don't listen."

"Why not?"

"Because they are stupid. How do I know why not?"

Mad maybe, but not stupid. To me everyone seemed mad. Everyone was neurotic, psychotic or some kind of a maniac in my opinion. The most ordinary people have Greek tragedies at home, and seemingly normal, healthy, sporty-looking males like Brösel are case histories. What the hell do you mean by "people" and "saints"? Phrases. Words. Empty references. Reality! Reality!! Only the touchable within the immediate surroundings seemed real. A railing that prevents you from falling into the sea and drifting beneath the waves is real.

8

Chairs and tables, cabin bunks are real. A deck is real. The gong. The food. To vomit is real. To sleep. Even dreams are real, as they take place in a real brain, inside a real skull, which I can hit against a real ceiling when the boat rocks. Reality was for me; the rest seemed madness. And even my "philosophy" of reality was nonsense and a trifle. My real problem was money, not reality. Ideas I had enough of. I thought Brösel was right: things have to be paid for. A warm place costs money, therefore thinking and pondering cost money, therefore writing costs money. Peace and relaxation are not cheap. And though it might be better to be poor and alive than rich and dead, even a poor existence has gone up in cost. Money is something spiritual as well. Gold is magic. People who had a lot of this magic during the war escaped from the guillotine and saved their necks, and to think of "the world" is just an attempt to forget that I can't pay for my own ticket to Amsterdam.

Money, money. I dreamed and thought of money and of nothing else all day and all night. Nothing else. Behind all philosophical systems, behind all artistic enterprises, was the sober fact that one needed money. All the dreams and illusions of this life have to be settled with hard cash.

"We are expecting a baby in July as well."

"I noticed. Go to Canada. It's wealthy."

"Wealth is evil! The wealthy are greedy—hyenas and dogs. Dog eats dog and man eats man in your system."

"Ordinary simple folks just like you and me—you can't call them hyenas and dogs, you snob."

"Me? A snob? You are the snob. You like to make money."

"No, you are the real snob. To earn money is the only universal occupation of every single human being everywhere

9

in the world. Except for saints. Saints are different. Saints can live on a piece of dry bread for weeks."

To whatever I said he had a twist. I believed in the virtue of the dispossessed. I was brought up on a diet of phrases such as: "Man is born good and free, but the State is evil. It turns a playful, modest, innocent soul into a cool, calculating, greedy monster. Yet survival is no end in itself."

Without Nazis and madmen after me, survival seemed a dull, uninspiring project.

The third evening on board was Passover. No bread, only matzos to eat. The tables in the dining room were joined and covered with white linen, silverware, specially polished plates, candles and flowers. A young man with thick glasses, a small yarmulke and a lisp like that of Moses himself presided over the mystical homecoming celebration of the old tale of how we were slaves in Egypt until God led us out with an outstretched hand and a hard fist. Jews have not only hard fists but also a good memory of the sweetness of peaceful humility among strangers. Only thinking of this exile, a number of old people who were making their last journey kept crying until it was time to drink four glasses of wine and join in the traditional song *"Be shana haba be Yerushalayim"* ("Next Year in Jerusalem").

"Not me," Brösel whispered. "They won't see me back so soon."

These singing and crying people dressed up in their finest garments and dancing the hora are definitely different from "others." Whether it's in their faces and passports or not, they are a weird, strange lot outside their own country.

"How could I live in exile?"

"How? Let's go down to the bar and have a drink and philosophize about it. I think you can live better among others than among us. We are throat-cutters."

We went to the bar, where I found Nancy Sokoloff.

Life was all about love. Every woman meant love. The best thing in life was to be in love. Love was not just a flea's hop for the next bite. Love was something for all occasions, for all situations in life. Showers are excellent locations for love. Holy cities and promised lands are inside Nancy Sokoloff but not permanent places to stay. Nancy was an anarchist from London. She was the first anarchist I had ever met. For Nancy everything was free and the freedom to love was her highest ideal.

It wasn't only money, the Jews, the communists, the world, freedom, the Nazis, acting, writing, and traveling I had on my mind. I looked at Ida's big stomach and was frightened of the unborn. My problem was not who would look after the child—my father-in-law, Ida or God Himself. My problem was inside my brain, where something didn't function as it should.

While Ida sat on the sun deck wrapped in blankets, staring into her own unknown future, and Fritz tried to seduce Nancy Sokoloff with his white teeth, I lay on my bunk, stared right above me and imagined myself as the empty space in a long stippled line of warriors, horsemen and nomads. Inside was neither Jew nor Gentile, neither male nor female, but all of them simultaneously, or the absence of all. Inside was something which could not speak for itself yet as it was in a constant state of change, without either a body or a soul. Identification perhaps with an unborn son due in July? I wasn't him, but myself yet unborn, which confused me as I

11

couldn't think where I could possibly be if not on a bunk on C deck. I am there, I presumed, but something in me isn't born yet—what, I absolutely could not figure out, and wanted to dismiss the whole thing as fantasy. It dawned on me gradually that I might still be in my own father's mind, just as my unborn son was in mine. In that case I am only an idea, nothing but an idea, but as an idea I definitely exist, though invisible to others and sometimes even to myself. How many circles will I have to go through to reach existence? I counted seven: doubt, fear, hesitation, consideration, projection, indecision, uncertainty. What chance did I have to be born into this world if the biologists are right and from the millions of small heads of sperm only one ever makes it? If a sevenfold shield protects one from becoming (which means birth for the unborn and death for the living), birth, I concluded, is neither necessary nor unavoidable, but happens all the same. Was the boat rocking me up and down? I felt distinctly that if it hadn't been for an incomprehensible force outside myself I would never have become. This self grows a body around itself. Does it first grow brain tissue or first the feet? I couldn't imagine myself to have been born without either, nor could I see all existence and nonexistence as a constant crossing from nothingness into something and back again and so on, which it is. I ate myself through ovum, placenta, womb and my mother, and if there had been more inside, I might never have come out. To have eaten my mother hollow just as I was eating my life up now was not a cheerful conclusion to come to.

In April '50 there was still peace in the world. Korea began a few months later. Peace. Peace. People coming and going from work, people window-shopping, people hanging onto

12

streetcars, milling along the Canebière, crowding around street vendors, listening to football matches over the radio (there was no TV yet), drinking coffee in the sun. People behind every window. World War I. Fifteen million dead. World War II. Forty-five million dead. And not a chance in sight to make a World War III. What's going to happen? I put the question to Mr. Bush, the Austrian vice-consul, a weird man with a small mustache, sad brown eyes and a slight limp, when we went to change ten dollars on the black market down at the harbor. I'd left Ida in the hotel room to rest and Brösel at the post office to cable his uncle in Montreal to send a hundred and fifty dollars to Vienna, in case Honig had forgotten.

"What's going to happen? What do you think?"

"Suicide. That's what's going to happen. The government will force everyone to commit suicide on the day of his retirement from work. Mark my words."

Private woe twisted back into a universal suffering becomes more interesting.

He was a Tyrolese Corsican, married, with six children, and maybe only thirty or thirty-two. His name he insisted was Elphants (and not Alphonse) Bush. When he saw *Actor* on my passport he believed I was the right company for him. He had finally found someone to talk to. He walked with a heavy leather briefcase glued to his right hand, an old tradition of French and Austrian civil servants. The briefcase was stuffed with bread, apples, books, newspapers, many pens and two or three writing pads; this too has its tradition. After we changed the dollars, he took me to a pockmarked elderly Moroccan who sat on his haunches and shuffled three cards for the game of Red Wins among a crowd of tourists, housewives with smelly fish in their shopping bags and children of all sizes and ages. He introduced me as an old friend from Israel and Vienna, at which the Moroccan commented dryly, "Red wins."

More than talking philosophy, even more than making love in shower rooms, I liked to gamble. Without a penny I couldn't take on responsibilities; even the smallest sums made me feel uneasy. I didn't know how to get rid of money fast enough. I liked to think about money, not to own it. I would have given the Moroccan every cent in my pocket just so I could say to Ida, "It's over. I have spent it all. Call your father in Amsterdam collect and tell him to send down a plane to fly you out."

After I lost five dollars of the ten I had just changed, Elphants dragged me away. I hadn't expected it. He walked me back to my hotel to fetch Ida for a coffee on the Canebière. He had proved his friendship by pulling me away from the game and now felt entitled to knock me down with his briefcase or press me through a shop window. The subject of art and literature made him nervous. "Sorry, I am so excited. Sorry. Excuse me. But you don't know . . . to meet a man like you . . . I never have a chance to talk to anyone. Nobody ever listens to me." In front of the hotel he suddenly gripped me at the top buttons of my shirt and nearly strangled me. "Fuck literature! *Merde, merde, merde. Scheisse.* Literature, fooey. Repeat after me: Fuck literature."

A crowd began to form around us and I finally struggled out of his grip.

"What's with you? Have you gone insane or has anyone refused your manuscript? Fuck literature; so what?"

He let me go and calmed down.

"I don't care if all the publishers in the world return my manuscript with mean and nasty letters. What really hurts is that deep inside I know myself to be the greatest literary genius in the world. I know it's a masterpiece. Do you understand? I don't think it's a masterpiece. I know it. It's the greatest novel since *Rouge et Noir*. The greatest. Yes. It's called 'Here, Now and Then.' "

"But I don't even know *Rouge et Noir*."

Elphants was so stunned at my shameless admission of my ignorance that his mouth fell open and he began shaking his head.

"You don't know *Rouge et Noir?* You don't know *Rouge et Noir?* Are you putting me on? Are you for real?"

"No. I don't read. I never read *Rouge et Noir*." I must have hit on something serious. "What's wrong with you, Elphants?"

He quite suddenly and unexpectedly turned his face into a grimace of blissful happiness and shrieked with laughter. "You are my true friend for life . . . you are my brother. Yes. My brother." He abruptly bent over and whispered, "I have stopped reading too. I destroy every book, or nearly every book. And you, my friend, are the only one who knows this; not even my wife knows this, my children do not know this, my father does not know this. All of them think I am reading, reading all the time. I lie to them. I have been lying to them for many, many years. The moment of truth has come. Here and now. Yes, sir. Thank you, thank you. It will be our secret and you will never tell anyone what you know. Swear."

"I swear."

He embraced me and kissed me on both cheeks. "We are friends from now on, inseparable friends. Our hatred for literature has welded a bond between us that nothing and no one can ever break. I swear this by the Father, the Son,

15

the Holy Ghost and Mary and by the life of my family."

Hardly arrived back in Europe, I had found a friend for life; he was insane and probably dangerous but at the age of twenty-three I collected nuts as Nabokov his butterflies. We fetched Ida and went for a Pernod and a coffee on the Canebière, leaving a note for Brösel in the hotel. Elphants started his soliloquy and never stopped. Every time Ida thought he wasn't looking in her direction she whispered in Dutch, "He is crazy; watch out." (She usually panicked with crazy people.) I watched for Brösel to rescue me from this situation I had got myself into. Fritz would know how to handle this one. He would shut him up with some talmudic bons mots.

Sitting in the sun on the Canebière, I felt happier than on the terrace of the Kassith in Tel Aviv. Is it because I don't understand French? The same feeling of being private in an isolated cell in a crowd kept me alive in Germany during the war years and here in Marseilles I had nothing to fear but a car when I crossed the road. To sit in the most beautiful town in the world drinking my coffee in the sun was a dream come true. What's more, not only did I do a stranger the favor of allowing him to pour out his mind and heart; I did myself an even better turn by learning to listen to other people's madness and forgetting my own for a while. (Had someone at this time suggested I should become a psychiatrist and paid for my study, I would have thought this the best of all solutions to all problems. Psychiatry seemed the right profession for me.)

Elphants Bush was not a Corsican Austrian, as he had told me at first, but a White Russian. A Turkmelian Tartar who

16

grew up first in Turkey and then in France. "I come from a country that cannot be found on any map. It just disappeared before they could put it there. It called itself the Turkmelian Republic and lasted maybe six weeks. We left in the very last moments, just an hour or two before the hetman Soloveitschik and his men rode into the town on their way to liberate the world. Everyone left; those who stayed had their right hands chopped off for collaborating with the Reds. My father, who is something of a professional collaborator, managed to empty the local bank and stuff it into two suitcases just in time. He sat on them and cinched the horses while my mother and my sisters prepared the two hand grenades we were taking along in case of trouble. We had hardly passed Trebizond when trouble started. Forty peasants blocked the road with sticks and red flags and wanted to see our papers. 'Give them the papers,' my father yelled, and my mother threw the grenades among the peasants. Seven blew up, three were badly wounded, the rest ran for their lives. I was wrapped in a bundle, sucking away at a piece of *moshin*—what they call poppies or opium. It's used to keep small children quiet. I learned before I knew what was going on in this world that half of life is good luck and the rest courage. We made it to the Turkish border just in time. The border was sealed by British and French interventionists and it cost us one of the suitcases of silver, gold and rubles to get through. But we made it. I went to a Turkish kindergarten in a Catholic Italian mission and grew up speaking Turkish and Italian. My father went into business with two Armenians selling German tourists guided tours to Noah's Ark on Mount Ararat. Of course, none of the Germans ever came down from the mountain; God knows what they did with them. Maybe my father was a bit of a decadent Tartar, but he

17

preferred a comfortable life in Ankara to the job of finance minister in our little stinking independent republic. My mother hated the Turks; she called them devils and wanted to move. Under a special exchange program that actually applied only to Greeks and Armenians, we moved first to Athens, then to Salonika, eventually to Trieste, and slowly, slowly kept moving west like swallows returning from a winter in the desert. I was twelve when we came to France in the middle of a strike and a crisis. There was nothing to do here for my father, so he went to Corsica and began to deal in crucifixes and other church utensils, and this went quite well for a while. He had a business contact in Trieste, two brothers called Fink who manufactured the stuff on the small island of Rab, off the Dalmatian coast, and smuggled it, evading all duties and taxes, to Corsica. But in 1934, after the assassination of the king of Yugoslavia in Marseilles, the police searched our house and discovered a ton of machine guns, dynamite and hand grenades in boxes marked crucifixes and Madonnas. My father went to jail for twenty years and would have stayed there had the Germans not bailed him out."

At this moment Brösel joined our table. He was introduced to Elphants, who was naturally deeply disturbed by the loss of attention.

"Carry on, carry on," Fritz said, showing his white teeth in the most stupid of all grins. How could anyone carry on a story with Fritz Brösel around grinning?

"What's happened? Excuse me, Elphants. He just sent a cable to Montreal for me. What's up?"

"Nothing. Absolutely nothing. But while I was waiting in the queue at the post office I picked up the most beautiful girl in the world. Swedish. You know what that means."

"Where is she? Why didn't you bring her along?"

"I'll see her tonight."

"We are taking the train tonight."

"We are taking the train tomorrow. Don't worry, I'll settle everything."

Life was getting exciting. Another night in Marseilles with Fritz, Elphants and Ingeborg, and Ingeborg must have a few girl friends in town. Suddenly I had quite a number of most important things to do. Get the life story of Elphants Bush, and Ingeborg when that was finished. I didn't know what to do first. Before anything else I had to make sure that Ida wouldn't mind going to bed early and only after I had solved that problem could I decide what to do first: listen to Elphants' story or go to town with the Swedish girls. After living five years in small towns, Marseilles at night surpassed my wildest dreams. Lights, everywhere lights. All places alight with people, music, prostitutes, gangsters. Dreamland of tingle-tangle. Fun fair. Merry-go-round. I floated seven feet above the crowds; I was back in a Prater paradise I had dreamed of since I left Vienna in '38. Everything was possible, everything could happen. To be alive for the sake of fun and pleasure and not because we came out alive from the gas chambers was the new thrill. There is no because, no gas chamber, no memory. It all happens now and requires no pious addresses to an archaic godhead of legendary ancestors, no lengthy pompous involved mysterious explanations, no need to wag the ethical index finger. Everyone knows it's not forever. Normal people laugh at it.

To have my heathen cake and yet not eat it was simple. I would wait down in the lobby of the hotel or maybe on

19

the first terrace, next to it, until Fritz brought one or two Ingeborgs; would get another story from my new-found character Elphants Bush; and would make Ida feel I hadn't left town, all at the same time. It seemed a brilliant solution.

Elphants left us at seven to go home for a quick change and a few words with his family. He came back punctually at ten-thirty, glad to see neither Ida nor Fritz around. He now had my undivided attention and tried to make the best of this windfall.

"What's opium like, Elphants?"

"Opium? Opium is good for the coolies. A man like me needs something better and stronger. Something that lifts your head and does not throw you down into the garbage."

"What's that?"

"Ergot."

"What?"

"Ergot. I'll tell you the whole story if you don't interrupt."

"Not even once?"

"Not even once. It's a bit complicated. It starts in Biot. Do you know Biot? It's a small town not far from here, just up on the hills between Vence and Cannes, off the main road. A pretty little town famous for Fernand Léger, who lived nearby.

"I told you my father—his name is actually Tibor but the English called him Tiger—is a professional collaborator. He serves only those in power. As a matter of principle. My mother claimed it's not the Tartar but the Austrian in him and the truth is there was an Austrian nobleman back in the seventeenth century, one of the early travelers and discoverers on his way to China, who dismounted from his camel in

Sochi on the Black Sea for a drink, fucked the daughter of an innkeeper and stayed. Their name was von Busznitzky, a good Polish German name such as so many Austrian aristocrats were settled with. Anyway, when Laval and Pétain took over, my father suddenly remembered that he had always detested the communists and everyone believed that as a White Russian he had every reason to hate their guts. Who was going to find out after all these years that he was the finance minister of a Red Turkmelian republic that lasted hardly two months? As he was the biggest busybody, with the most money and connections, he ended up as mayor of the town. He was not a Nazi—hell, no—he was just a good anticommunist because Laval ran the unoccupied part of France. To be a foreigner and a mayor of a small town in France, even with French nationality, he had to prove himself in Vichy. He had to produce results. And he did. No Jew, communist or anarchist was safe within a hundred miles of Biot. If he denounced a man, he wasn't satisfied that the police might or might not get him. The police was riddled with maquis; he had to make the arrests himself. And if people drew guns on him, he proved to be quicker on the draw. How many he killed and maimed we never found out, but it's enough to tell you that he never left the house without the five-man bodyguard he paid out of his own pocket. Hired locals. We were not allowed to leave the house. The streets were not safe for us; he was afraid we would be shot as soon as we set foot out of doors. It wasn't easy, believe me. But what could I do? I couldn't afford five Marseillais gangsters to protect me, and to make sure we would never leave the house the old man took all our shoes away. We were his prisoners in a golden cage. He provided the foie gras, caviar and champagne. We even had our own movies at home.

L'éternel Retour by that other collaborator Jean Cocteau is one I remember. To come to the point: On a Saturday morning, the fourteenth of July, day of the Republic, the noise in the street was different, a totally different kind of noise. I'll try to describe to you what it was like."

"Just a moment; hold your horses. The story is getting too long."

Elphants gave me a nasty look. I believed there was something dangerous in his eyes. Suddenly I was frightened. While only an hour or so ago he had seemed to fit in so well with my various plans for the evening, I now saw in him a rogue, charlatan and cheat, no longer the madman literary genius of the same afternoon who had nearly strangled me because he thought I loved publishers. The danger was not physical, nothing I could define. It was the feeling of being carved open and filleted and stuffed with words. This was going on far too long, with no Brösel in sight and no phone call. I didn't want to go up and wake Ida, nor did I want to go to bed. I couldn't very well suddenly get up and walk away, and I had the feeling he would follow me wherever I went anyway. I regretted ever having spoken to him and felt like the fool I was, to let him get so close. Ida was right after all: Bush is a dangerous maniac who preys on innocent travelers and kills them with a barrage of never-ending words.

"Do you want to listen or don't you want to listen? I was just about to come to the point where the whole town went insane because they ate bread with poisoned rye. People tore off their clothes in the street. They shat and pissed, fucked and danced and howled like animals gone mad, until the police and the fire brigade arrived and carried them off to God knows where."

"Please come to the point. The way you tell a story it'll last all night."

"I'm nearly finished. I saw the liquefaction of the flesh with my own eyes. People dissolved into weird monsters. I'll never forget the old woman, the wife of the carpenter."

"What did she do?"

"She cracked her head open against a wall. Her brains fell out."

"Yes; all right. So people went mad because they ate poisoned bread. So what?"

"So what? A whole loaf of this bread ended up in our house and I still don't understand how."

"So your family went mad too."

"Wrong again. My father wanted to burn the bread, but I snatched it from him, locked myself up in my room. By the time he had broken down the door I had eaten the whole *baguette*."

"What happened?"

"How do I know what happened? I still don't know. Don't you see what I'm getting at? I don't know. I don't know anything. All I remember is an American or two in uniform and a number of maquis entering our house and taking the family away."

"Why didn't they take you away?"

"They were afraid of me. I sat curled up in a cupboard and bit everyone who came near me."

"What happened to the family?"

"They shot them, except my old man."

"Why not your old man—wouldn't they shoot him first?"

"They couldn't. My father, it turned out, had been head of the maquis at the same time."

"I thought he was the man who murdered the maquis."

23

"Both. Their leader and their executioner. Those who didn't want to believe he was both died."

"Listen, Elphants, that's too much. You give me a headache. How do you invent all these things?"

"I don't invent anything; it's the absolute truth. Why don't you come and meet the old Tiger?"

He stared into my eyes and I stared back at him. There was nothing I could say. I wanted to get out.

"Let's meet tomorrow. I'm going to bed now."

"Aren't you waiting here for Fritz and the girls?"

"No, I'm going to bed. I don't want to wait any longer. Good night."

"Have I offended you? Have I said anything wrong? Please forgive me. I didn't mean it; I didn't mean it."

He became pathetic and made me feel sorry for his destroyed mind. Bush obviously lived in a real darkness; he was not just a man who fed my mania for collecting stories, but truly a wretched soul who needed help. Maybe I could do or say something and save him with a few good words. I couldn't think of anything to say. A storm seemed to have blown away my paradise and I gazed into a darkness I had never seen before. In front of my eyes Elphants turned into a small fluorescent insect dying in slow agony. I shook his hand to say good-bye. It was cold and lifeless. I saw tears in his eyes. Suddenly I got mad and yelled. "Fuck off, Elphants Bush! Go to hell! Go away! Run! Don't come back!" The last thing I heard before I went upstairs was his very softly spoken words: "I thought you were my brother." He limped away without turning around and disappeared in the crowd.

Fritz never showed up and I went upstairs. The rest of the night I compared Elphants to myself. Couldn't see the difference between his compulsion to say anything that came into his diseased mind and my own insane desire to listen to everyone who had a story to tell.

So far all had gone not too well. Fritz was having an orgy with all the Swedish hustlers in town while I wasted my time with a ridiculous mental case. I had thought I finally escaped the people chosen for suffering but realized that the mad are truly a universal family. I was back in a real world, and sooner than I had expected.

The season had just started. People sat in the sun all the way from Marseilles to Menton. On chairs and benches, pebbles and railings, and under white sails out in the blue sea. The apocalypse had been and gone; no angels flew safe above golden clouds, just kites. No one was sent to eternal hell by artillery and firing squads, though some people were forced to live in Nissen huts and shacks and overcrowded tenements. The palms and bushes burned with orange, red, yellow and purple and were free for all. Models, hairdressers, businessmen and soldiers sat on top of open cars and paraded along, an endless promenade of colors, flags and musicians, so everyone could see that the big war was finally over and finished once and for all. I wanted to pull the emergency cord. To get off right here in Cagnes-sur-Mer. I saw a house I fancied set in a huge green garden of pines and olives on top of a hill. The money for rent I could (with a bit of luck) make in the casinos of Cannes, Nice and Monte Carlo. I'd have chosen to be a pimp, gangster, waiter or boyfriend of rich old ladies rather than go back to the lower depths of Jewish middle-class Amsterdam. I'd have lived in a dream rather than return to my own reality at the terminal of this excursion. Why continue on this sentimental railroad track? I wondered. In twenty years the boulevards will be over-crowded, with no place to put up so much as a tent. Why not stay when land and houses are still going cheap? Why not? I had to do first things first. I remember a strange conversation on the train to Ventimiglia. We stood at the window and blocked the passage for everyone.

"What do you really want to do—what is your aim?"

"I want to be the first foreign president of the United States."

"Are you any good at politics?"

"Last time, I tried to organize thirty unemployed in Na-thanya to see the mayor and protest and only two showed up for the march through the main street. One of them left halfway through for his dental appointment and the other one persuaded me that it made no sense if only the two of us went it alone. I held the flag but no one walked behind me."

"How is your English?"

"Who needs English to be president of the United States? Anyway, Ida won't let me."

Ida stood suddenly behind me. "You can do whatever you like."

"I can't."

"Why not?"

"I can't, but I'll have to. I'd rather leave than destroy you."

"When are you leaving?"

"Not before the child is born."

"Why don't you leave now?"

"You want me to jump out of the window? I don't want to kill myself."

"But you don't mind destroying me?"

"Did I say that?"

"Yes, you did," said Fritz. "I heard you saying it. Why do you drive her crazy?"

"I have nothing else to do in my life. I don't want to talk about it. Let's go back to our *couchette*, Ida. I don't want him to listen."

How could we ever separate? I knew no woman better than Ida in bed and I was the man of her life. We could make love twenty-four hours a day; just couldn't talk about anything in between.

"She loves me and I love her, Fritz; that's the truth. She is all I have, I am all she has. Can you see our tragedy?"

Fritz grinned and said, "You are really a romantic ass. You surprise me."

I surprised myself. The way I stuck to her was somewhat stupid. Next morning in the restaurant car Fritz wanted to know everything again.

"How often did you make it with her last night?"

"None of your business. Let's discuss Canada instead."

"O.K. Canada. I have a cousin in Canada who makes movies. He started three years ago and now makes a lot of money."

"What's your cousin's name?"

"What does it matter?"

"Because with my name I couldn't even be a garbage collector."

"What's wrong with it?"

"It's too good for anything. My father was a Tartar king and my mother a duchess. I was born to live in a castle with a moat and wouldn't let your cousin and your uncle cross my drawbridge."

"What's wrong with being a film cutter?"

27

"What's wrong with being a duke? I have to divorce myself from the bourgeoisie. Afterward anything is possible. She thinks I am right for her. She must be crazy. I can't live with a crazy woman."

"What about you?"

"I wouldn't mind going to a loony bin for a while. It's free board and lodging and would give me the time to think and write."

The green uniform of the Austrian police without a swastika made me feel a bit better right away. The same uniform, the same faces, the same voices, and no swastika in sight. No Heil Hitler, no outstretched arms. Polite policemen saluted three dead Jews returning from their graves. One felt it clearly in the crisp mountain air of the Semmering: Jews are now more than welcome. (Come back, Jews. We have forgiven and forgotten everything! It was a big misunderstanding! We never hated you! We never wanted whatever happened to happen!) The train was held up for an hour, engines were changed, we stretched our legs on the platform, walked around. No board that said: FÜR JUDEN VERBOTEN. Anyone who pays good currency can now eat the Austrian specialties *Topfntatschkerlnpowidlgolatschn* here. The Hitlers come and go. Who cares whether they wanted it or not? It just happened. In one side of the oven and out the other. Congratulations, you clever Jews! Why didn't you tell your brethren how to do this? Then we wouldn't have that bad reputation we now have in the world.

I had come back as a spy and secret agent of a superpower to blow up what was left of my childish recollections and leave by the next train. But not before we found Honig.

28

Who was this Honig? What was his business? Do people exist with a name like "Honey"? We tried every coffeehouse. Fritz came with me. Neither in the synagogue, nor in the Gartenbau, nor at Spritzer had anyone ever heard of him. It looked as if Brösel might have to give me the hundred and fifty dollars from Montreal. As he didn't like the idea, he tried even harder than I to identify our Honig among all the hundreds of dealers in dollars, Swiss francs, nylons, needles and paper. Spare parts for heavy machinery were the best deal, as the Russians dismantled every piece of machinery the Americans had not flattened. Unlike us, the Russians wanted back what they had lost in the war. I only wanted to get out as soon as possible. We nearly found him at Mandel. "That gentleman over there," said the waiter, "might help you." He sent us to a man about sixty with an enormous paunch, wearing trousers that were too short but would fit if he'd lose weight. He wore a gray suit, a dirty white shirt with curled collar and a flowery tie. His face was white, his cheeks and eyes sagging; he looked like a white owl. He had maybe three of his own teeth; the rest were silver and gold. This indicated a Rumanian, but it turned out Julius Grünbaum was from Budapest and belonged to the postwar wave. The prewar originals, the "real Viennese," as far as could be seen, were in the more profitable wood and paper business. Grünbaum had watches, gold, diamonds, coffee, penicillin, morphine and "anything else you want." I began to understand why my father had never had a chance to make a penny in Vienna after the crash of '29. In the Vienna coffeehouses there were too many Grünbaums and he was a schlemiel compared to them. He should not even have tried to make small deals with these big toothless sharks. One has to speak their language. I just listened.

"I have this ring with two diamonds, one for you and one for your friend," Grünbaum said to Fritz.

"My friend has no money; he looks for a man called Honig, who should have money for him."

"Which Honig? Isidor Honig?"

"Do you know him?"

"Of course I know him. He is an honest man. Whose money is it, your money or your friend's money?"

"It's money from his father-in-law."

"Who is his father-in-law?"

"His father-in-law lives in Amsterdam."

"Take this ring for a hundred dollars. It's worth a thousand. Do yourself a favor."

"What kind of ring is it?"

"It belonged to the mother of Count Pototsky. Is that good enough?"

"All right. Let's go."

"Wait a minute, young man. What's the hurry? Think. Don't hurry. What do you want in life?"

I looked at Grünbaum, but Grünbaum had addressed Brösel, not me.

"Whom do you ask, him or me?"

"Him"—he nodded at me with his gray hat (he never took it off, he must be in business with the Orthodox, I decided)— "him I don't even want to ask. He is insane. He just runs around in circles and doesn't know what he wants." Grünbaum had hit the nail right on the head. "But you, you look like someone who knows what he wants. What do you want, I'd like to know?"

"The same thing."

I didn't know why he said it and didn't know what he meant by "the same thing." Did he mean he wanted to be a professional intellectual, whatever that may be? Then he was wrong; that's not what I wanted. I wanted to have time to write, but I didn't want to belong to the intellectuals. I didn't like them, didn't feel they were my kind of people (a feeling that hasn't changed much over the years). I never read a book at that time and was not really interested in literature or acting. I said, "If you want the same thing as I you must want to be God."

"Why not? Why not want to be God? What does it cost to want to be God? Whatever the prize, I want the same thing."

We walked from the Schwedenbrücke to the Praterstern, the entire length of the bombed-out Praterstrasse. I smelled the familiar perfume of floor polish, ice cream, damp clothes and Bulgarian rose water the tarts of this beat trail behind them to drive small schoolboys insane. We passed the Tegethoffdenkmal and walked along the wooden fences to the right of the Lassallestrasse, my former way home from Tuesday evening swims in the Dianabad. Ennsgasse 13 had for some miraculous reasons survived air bombardments and the artillery of the Russians with hardly any damage. Gray green, tall, with a hundred windows overlooking the hothouses of the city council and the mysterious high fence of a building site on the corner of Ybbsstrasse . . . I asked Fritz to let me climb on his back to have a look over the fence.

"If it's fenced in, it means you shouldn't see it."

"That's what my mother said."

"She was right."

I decided to ring the doorbell and who knows, maybe the present tenants would be kind enough, if I explained who I was, to let me, now I'm taller, look from our windows to see what's across the fence. I had not expected our own Mitzi from Hadres to open the door, clutch me to her big soft white breasts and put me right up her white soft thighs; nor had I expected to face a toothless, tiny ninety-year-old woman. I repeated my name, added I was born here and had come to ask permission to be allowed, that is if she wouldn't mind, et cetera, to give one quick look across the fence from the window.

"Born here? *Ja. Ja.*"

She repeated my name a few times and finally gave me a grin.

"I knew your parents. I used to live upstairs on the fourth floor. What happened to them?"

"They died."

"Poor people, and they were so very nice. I remember your Herr Vater and your Frau Mutter very well. Very nice, very good people."

"Can I come in and look around?"

"That's a little difficult. You see, I'm a very old woman and I live alone."

She didn't trust me; she was afraid I'd come to throw her out and ask for the apartment back. You never know with Jews nowadays, the Viennese said in '50; they are capable of doing anything. Now they have the law on their side.

"Another time maybe. Good-bye."

She turned three locks. There won't be another time, I said. This was definitely my last attempt to reenter the womb.

"Why didn't you bash her head in with a hammer like Raskolnikov if you really want to go back to the cradle? Or fuck her; she would let you have a room, marry her and when she dies you get the place and you are back. Where do you want us to go now?"

"I want to see the Goethehof across the bridge, where I grew up. Ennsgasse I don't really remember. I was two when we moved."

"Still haven't had enough?"

"No. It's cheaper to take line twenty-four across the bridge than see a psychiatrist. Everyone should try to go back to his origins. I don't know why. I've waited twelve years for today, to see who lives in number twenty-five, second floor, door number nine."

Novak, Werner, Hubalek, Pitschinger, Senft, Platschek, and for number 9 it said: Krapfinger. I walked up three flights, stood in front of our door and wanted to ring the bell, but what would I say this time if someone opened? I came to look at the white coal box in the kitchen? Are the nymphs and fauns still over the bed? May I look for my playing cards? Where the hell am I, what kind of world is this I have come back to? I must have died somewhere inside when I left this house in the summer of '38 and I move in an underworld now. The white paint on the door and the polished chrome of the nameplate made me feel dizzy and I left town, crossing the Danube from east to west on the last leg of this visit through the underworld. I passed four more stations.

Wohlmutstrasse 8, where the Breindlers lived, was a bomb crater; Erlafstrasse 11, where we had our club, a dentist's; Mumsplatz 5, where my first love, Berta Beller, lived and where, under a chestnut tree diagonally opposite number 5, I had made my first (and last) marriage proposal, at the age of eleven. Her mother said she would have to wait until she was sixteen.

"Did you ever make it with her?"

"Make what?"

"Finger her? Suck her tits?"

"At eleven?"

"We had a boy in the class who fucked his aunt at ten. At eight my mother found me in the basement inside an empty barrel with three girls. I had my fingers in two of them and the third one blew me. All that without marriage proposals. You must have been hung up on your respectable mother. You are a bourgeois! You are no existentialist!"

"I told you, I don't even know what that is."

The Prater, as everyone had told me beforehand, was an empty, dirty, bombed-out place. Nothing. No stalls, no stages, no slot machines, no Lilliputians, no sawn-in-half ladies, no fat Mitzis. Nothing, nothing. No ghost train, no grotto train, no Flick and Flock. Nothing. Nothing. Old ladies walking their old dogs on leashes. Lonely drunken old men walking in deep silence with heads bent like at a funeral. Nothing. It's all finished. No one-legged dwarfs, no women without arms and legs, no double-headed pygmies, no giants, no Frankenstein monsters, no ghosts. Gone, gone forever. Don't come close, ladies and gentlemen, keep your money. There is nothing to see. There is no attraction and no sensation, neither inside nor outside nor anywhere else! Go home, ladies and gentlemen. Everyone is dead!

I had seen it all and there was no more to be seen. I had made the final crossing back into the womb and all that was left to do was try to get out. When we came back Ida was still on the bed, resting. She had been worried and was happy to see me alive. She loved me. Honig had come and gone.

34

After paying the hotel bill and the fare, we should still have five dollars left, which was enough for coffee on the train.

Fritz took us to the station the next morning, helped with the luggage and stood on the platform alone and lost. We exchanged addresses, promised to write one another, I would visit him in Canada or he would come to Amsterdam, somehow get together again. It never happened. I never saw him again.

Anyplace where people gathered I met someone to talk to, and even the greatest idiot or most miserable creep had a story to tell; if they weren't all as insane as Elphants Bush, there was always some element of interest to them. "I am studying life," I said. The others called it bumming and fucking around. The town seemed to have no other topic of conversation and my reputation wrapped me into a not altogether undesirable isolation. I actually preferred those who didn't like me to those who did, as they left me alone. Most of my "friends" found me entertaining: I was a strange egg in their nest, a foreigner who had returned from Israel as a temporary visitor to tell stories in order to ensnare their women. True, I looked for friendly female souls to console me in my difficult days. Afraid to start anything on my own and not knowing exactly what it was I wanted, except to hang around, I needed a woman to look after me. And as love produces chain reactions, I soon had a great number of female friends whom I adored and loved. Each one separately, each one because of her own beauty and virtue, each one because she was different and unique. And the entire species of women put together was a strange mutation of flower and butterfly

in my eyes. Just by touch they could magic me (or my kind—
men) into something else. I called them adventures of the
mind. Every woman I met had her own sphere, her own identity, her own love, and I couldn't say the same for my male
friends who drank with me until all hours of night and day.
With one or two exceptions, I liked the females not only for
friends and for spending time in bed with, but also for general good feelings that strengthen the body and soul; women
and only women are better. In spite of the dragons among
them, they create peace, a peace that does not have to be
dull but fills you entirely until everything you touch and
think is affected by it. To have a good woman is one of the
really divine blessings next to good health. Love when ex-
perienced that way causes reverberations that are unpredict-
able in their ultimate effect.

The more you love the less you should, is a strange kind of
love, in which most people believe. The more I loved the more
I loved—and if I could have had them all I wouldn't have
minded losing one or two; but as I couldn't have them all
(some lived physically too remote from my stamping
grounds), I caused within my limited orbit all kinds of trouble. When I was still in love with the woman I was now about
to divorce (to gain an illusory freedom) I was also in love
with her girl friends Rena and Miriam. When I met Dinah I
fell in love; when I met her best girl friend, Marijke, I was
lost. Dinah was beautiful and dark, Marijke beautiful and
light; the first Jewish, the second Gentile; the one full of mind,
the other full of soul. Of course the two belonged together and
loved each other, but they had to share me. This had to happen secretly; they were not supposed to know. They were
both nineteen and had grown up in the very decent, respectable liberal soil of Bussum, a small town twenty miles

southeast of Amsterdam, famous for its chocolate and its deft burghers. In Bussum my privacy was invaded in May 1940 by a German parachutist who one day jumped out of the clear sky and destroyed irreparably the freedom of Eden. What was left of it were the two forces of dark and light, called now Dinah and Marijke.

The newborn was due very soon, but instead of looking for an apartment and a job I came home every morning, slept until lunch and disappeared into the town again. I had nothing to say anyway. My case was clear. She and her family knew that all I wanted was to get out and away as soon as possible, but was waiting for the baby to be born so as not to embarrass them. (It also gave me a permanent address with a family of respectable middle-class people.)

Had the Holy One, blessed be His name, who commanded the Jews to circumcise their newborn told me personally I should allow this to happen to my very own son, I might have agreed. As far as I was concerned, a new baby should be neither Jew nor Christian, Arab nor Hindu, but just a human being. *Ein Mensch.* I refused permission. At least for a short time, maybe a week or two. I thought the clan really cared what I had to say on this issue. "He is not to be circumcised. I don't want it." Alex, my brother-in-law, stepped back for more effect. This madness incarnate needed objective distance. I knew Alex wanted to talk about it. "Listen, Alex. I want out of it. I want to have nothing more to do with your lower-middle-class Jewish family. I was born among them. I can't stand them. I want out. Of course it's my arrogance, whatever you say, but I want out and I don't want my son to be forced into this tribe."

37

"Go on!" said Alex.

"The Jewish lower classes have to be Orthodox or Zionist or they will disappear. They can't think for themselves, but my mother appointed me to be a doctor—that means be smarter than the others. I feel free to deny any law and any command of God. The truly God-fearing are more heretic, as they are higher, and any child of mine is a *mensch* first and a Jew afterward."

"You are an interesting case," said Alex, "but all the same, a boy must be circumcised, come what may."

"You are insane. I don't have to be a Jew—I am one already! Don't you understand? I can deny what I like!"

"But as you are a Jew, you must circumcise him."

"No, Alex, I don't have to do anything of the kind. You can do it by force and you probably will, but I am against it as a matter of principle. In the days of masses an elite has only a small chance to survive. But why commit us at birth to it? Why not let a person make his free decision when he is grown up and can choose?"

"Why? If you wait for Jews to choose to be Jews, you can wait a long time. Don't you know that?"

"So who needs Jews?"

"Why do you ask me? Ask Him."

"Listen, Alex. The next son I might circumcise, but not this one. Yet I love him as much as I can love my son. I'd probably love him even more if I could have it my way."

"My family, as if to make sure your madness would not disturb us good Jews, believes in a sentence that says: 'Let us die rather than transgress the commands of the God of our fathers.' You understand what I am getting at? My father would die of grief if you had it your way."

"All right, just carry on with your blackmail. Very well

then, I'll ask God. God! Yes? Do you want me to have Grischa circumcised? Yes or no? Do what you like. You hear what He says? Do what you like. That's the way to get a quick reply."

"But that's not the way to ask God," Alex said. "Look at this." He went to the cupboard where he kept between the china and the silver a small velvet bag. He took out a tallith, put on his tfilin, opened a small prayerbook and began to shake forward, backward, occasionally making a little side-step, and all the time rattling something with such incredible speed that it ultimately came out like a high humming sound. Suddenly he stopped in this sound and shouted, *"Adonai. Achod!*

"Did you see? That's the only way He listens."

He packed up his utensils, put them back in their silk and locked them away.

"What did He say to you, Alex?"

"He said: Tell your brother-in-law to lose some of his intelligence and get *sechel*, the Jewish brand of intelligence, instead."

"Thank you."

"Talk to Him again, talk as long and as much as you like. Talk until you get blue in your face. We'll cut him, we certainly will, on the eighth day, even if you jump out of the window. First comes the law—I mean my father's health."

The blood flowed from a small fountain of heavenly delights. All people present, enraptured with pleasure, shouted, *"Mazel tov!* Another one of us! *Mazel tov!"* They came up to congratulate me. I don't know what for: for having lost my arguments against tradition or for having acquired a new member of the Kahal Israel, a notion of Jewish community

39

and brotherhood nearly as holy as the Blessed One who commands circumcision.

Fondling and smoking were not yet in. Existentialists, intellectuals and businessmen, artists and prostitutes had these two things in common: fuck as much as you can and drink as much as you can hold. In these good old days, it seems to me, when people owned no more than a bicycle and thanked God for that, the pursuit of pleasure was much greater than now. I had to get out of Amsterdam or drop dead in a chair at Eylders, poisoned by Jenever and beer. The drinking was good everywhere—at Reinders and in the Kring—only at Eylders, where there was less space to move, both sex and booze could be consumed simultaneously, which saved a lot of time for more of the same. I thought it was time to leave this kind of existence, and thought of Paris, not too far and not too near, as a reasonable spot to continue where I would leave off here. I had in my pocket a letter from the Israeli director Peter Frye that might get me into the École Cinématographique. With a railway ticket and three hundred dollars from my father-in-law, I had to see for myself five years later, now that the Gare du Nord had stopped unloading ex-concentration camp inmates, if there was anyone in Paris who would prevent me from returning to Amsterdam. I found a room on the third floor of the American House of the Cité Universitaire. The regular students were away on holiday. I remember climbing the stairs, I remember lying down on the bed, but I can't remember that I ever fell asleep. Nor was I eager to wake out of these d.t.'s. Awake I might have gone back to Amsterdam and my son. How long one could remain in a state of d.t.'s without fading away was a matter of body over mind. There was no doctor around and no one to put

40

food through my veins. I was neither hungry nor thirsty, though I hadn't eaten for days. When I finally got out of bed, did I expect a crowd of people around to applaud it? The room was empty. The voices I had heard all the time must have spoken to me from another dimension. It was late August and hot. Very hot. The Cité Universitaire was open, but the rest of Paris was closed except for American tourists, who ate all night and sang all morning. (There were only American tourists; others didn't have the money to travel.) I couldn't join them. All I could do was watch old men playing chess in a little café off the Boulevard Saint Michel or, in the Jardins du Luxembourg, look at girls reading books and shelling peanuts and children playing with their boats under the fountain. I wandered through museums, stared into the river and spent many hours on the terraces of the Select, Deux Magots and Flore, watching people. I had spent every penny and didn't quite know what to do next. I knew no one in Paris. I met a girl on a chair next to mine who looked alone and lost like myself and she introduced me to the *maladie américaine,* the poverty of the rich.

"Texas is on the other side of the world. A big country with people who own horses, cattle, oil and money. You only know about the rich people in Texas, right? But most people in Texas, let me tell you, are black and poor, the grandchildren of slaves. Texas is where I was born. We always had money but I am ashamed of it. I wish I was born in France and my father was a Gypsy. By the way, my name is Lin."

"Why do you want to be poor and a Gypsy? Don't you like to be rich, Lin?"

"It's comfortable but I don't like it. If you have money it's hard to have anything else, right?"

41

"And if you don't have money?"

"I don't know what it is like to have no money. I always had money."

"Has your family never been poor?"

"Not that I remember."

"Where do you live?"

"In the Cité Universitaire."

"That's where I live. Which building?"

"American."

"That's where I live. You should be able to afford something better."

"What's better than living cheap?"

"Are you stingy?"

"I'm not crazy if that's what you mean."

"Which room are you in?"

"Three-o-four."

"I'm in three-o-five. If you pay for the taxi, we can take one together."

In the long ride through the dead town I looked at her: pretty dark hair and pretty blue eyes, beautiful mouth, perfectly shaped body—perfect like a wax model in a shop window. She was the first all-plastic American I had ever met. She smelled clean, well protected; she smelled of Bussum, of warm centrally heated houses, good food and lilac soap. She dressed like a cheap whore and yet was obviously hard to get. She seemed ideal. I wanted to marry her right away. She was rich and I thought she could afford a young starving genius for a few years, or at least over the next winter.

"Are you married?"

"No. Of course not. Are you?"

"Yes."

"Where is your wife?"

"I don't know. She is looking for me."

"Have you left her?"

"Yes."

"Why?"

"She bored me and loved me. She looked after me too well."

"Do you have money?"

"No."

"Does she have money?"

"Not that I know of."

"What do you do?"

"I repair the universe. It fell to pieces and I am picking them up."

"Is that your business?"

"Maybe it is. I have nothing else to do."

"What do you want to do?"

"I'm looking for time."

"Don't you have time?"

"I have no time. I have to write a book. I'm like Bush, a man I met in Marseilles."

"Who is Bush?"

"That's me."

"Is that your name? You said something else before."

"Before I was joking. I am Fred Bush."

"Who?"

"Never mind. You won't understand. It's a long story."

"Tell it."

"I'll tell it another time."

I wanted her to come to my room, where I would have told her anything she wanted to hear, but she was afraid,

43

probably worried I might turn out to be too expensive. Little did she know that I would have sold myself for less than five dollars a day, and if necessary only for bed and breakfast.

I left Paris after three weeks. With geese and peasants in the same compartment, I ate bread and cheese bought with my last two francs and was watched suspiciously by both peasants and geese while I looked with envious eyes at their fields and farmhouses. Lucky people, those peasants. They really know how to live well. The secret of life, I hoped to believe one day, was to stay in one and the same spot and never move beyond the last house of your village. I left the train at Soissons and began my long march to Amsterdam. I walked up and down many hills until a twelve-ton truck stacked high with rabbit skins picked me up. I must have fallen asleep immediately.

I sit on a horse. The sun sets behind violet mountains on the horizon and I am tired. It's late. I see a brook to the left and can smell the water. Out of nowhere rises a small house under trees. A water mill irrigates melons and eggplants. A woman stands suddenly behind me. I have my face in the water and drink next to my horse. I wash my face and hands, throw water down my neck and dry myself with the end of my shirt. I lie down and look at the sun setting in purple and gold. I fill a pipe and light it and think: This is the end of the world. I mustn't stay too long; my friends are far ahead of me. I must go. I must keep moving or I'll never catch up with them. I must go. I must, must, must. The woman sits next to me, looks me up and down and says, "Why don't you come in?" She has a pleasant voice; she is not beautiful but I like her big brown eyes. She has a slight squint; it doesn't really matter. I wonder whether she knows it.

"I have made food for both of us. Come in."

I am curious; I don't quite understand where I am. This hut wasn't here last time I passed this place. Where did it suddenly come from? I know her. She looks familiar and I can't think of her name. Either she is the sister of someone I know or a close friend of this sister. But I know that I know her. At the door she takes my boots off. The hut is small. High above us beams disappear in an attic without a roof. The place is small but has a few nooks and corners which might lead anywhere. Under a green lamp a big table, a few chairs, a bench, an oven, shelves full of plates and cutlery, pots and pans. On each of the four walls a picture: Adam and Eve in paradise with the snake and the apple; Cain killing Abel; Noah and his animals entering the ark; Abraham sacrificing Isaac. She must have cut them out of an illustrated prayer-book. The walls are made of fir. The floor is highly polished. It smells good.

"Who are you?"

"I live here." She ladles soup from a pot into a plate, cuts a thick slice of rye bread and watches me while I eat. I look at her. She smiles, reads my mind, hands me salt and pepper. She takes a huge side of beef from the same pot and cuts two slices off, puts them on my plate together with a hunk of bread and grated horse-radish. The meat needs more salt as well; the horse-radish is O.K. I belch. She smiles again. I have been in this scene before, I know it, but can't think of it.

"You live here by yourself?"

"Yes."

"No family, no husband?"

"No."

"Strange."

"What's strange? I expected you."

"Since when?"

"Quite some time."

She brings me tea and apple pie, takes my socks off, washes my feet in warm water and dries them with a towel. I fill a pipe, light it up and smoke. She takes the pipe out of my hand, draws a few times and gives it back. She looks into my eyes, smiles and I smile back.

Her body is very white. She has big breasts, big nipples, wide thighs, a large and firm body which smells of birch. She steps into bed, draws the blanket up to her face and watches me. I throw my things on the floor and step into bed. We talk and fuck and laugh. Cool spiced air comes through the open window. I like it here. I fall asleep with her head on my chest and my right thigh squeezed between hers.

The sun is high. It's hot; must be nearly noon. I dress and wash. My woman leans on her left elbow. "Your horse is gone. You might as well stay here." My horse is gone? The horse is gone, seems to have torn itself away from the rope. I can't believe it. I am angry. "Look what you did."

"I didn't do it; it just wanted to join its friends. You like it here or you would walk away."

"I can't walk."

"In that case you'd better stay."

"But I will hate you."

"One day you will love me for making you come down from your horse."

"You must be Jewish."

"I am."

"Are you my mother?"

"Right."

"It's incest. God will punish us."

"Love is what matters, not laws."

"What shall I do here?"

"There is always something to do."

"I can only ride horses."

"In time you'll learn something else."

"See this line from the middle of the triangle to the navel?" I see a dark line of hair from pubic triangle to navel. "That's a son. A line is a son. No line a daughter."

"A son with my own mother?"

"And your own son and grandson at the same time."

"God help us."

"He did."

I cut a navel string, make a knot, take hot water and wash the blood off her thighs. I can't believe it. A perfect child. "You too had blue eyes when you were born. Now hold the baby. Male children must be circumcised."

"It's barbaric," I shout. "Why cut a little child's flesh?"

"It's our kind of bond with God.'

What a terrific God she has! Sharp like a razor.

A child screams, blood spatters over the walls, trickles onto the yellow floor. She takes him to her breast, stuffs a nipple longer than his penis into his mouth. The baby drinks and falls asleep.

A cruel God, but He seems to provide plenty. Potatoes, eggplants, vegetables, fruit. A garden surrounded by an abundance of water. I work the garden, sleep in a hammock, play chess and dominoes and smoke pipes with her. I'm happy.

47

I'm glad I lost the horse. I lie on the bed, the baby sleeps next to me. She peels apples, boils them with sugar, fills jars with it. She talks to the baby, talks to me. I can't move from the bed, stare into the blue. She sings, the baby babbles, all is well. It's time to leave. What would she say if I suddenly left? I wouldn't be here to know. It's better to leave without a word.

I get up from the bed, take my boots, my coat and hat, and leave without turning back. For twenty miles I expect her to run after me, with or without the child. As nothing happens I carry on, and keep walking while she seems not to care one way or the other.

When I came back, there was nothing I could say to cheer Ida up. She had no mind left. She screamed and hated me. Even bed wouldn't do the trick. Nothing could ever repair this broken vessel.

After Paris I couldn't see any point in going anywhere but back to Paris. My father-in-law, who regarded his daughter's marriage as his personal failure in life, found us a place in Bussum. Bussum was no longer paradise, but hell. There was nothing wrong with the world, there hardly was "a world" I could observe, but this "I" within myself didn't know what to do. I tried to see any semblance of purpose in what was happening and I couldn't. I was certainly in love with Dinah and Marijke and with Amsterdam, yet strangely interested in neither Dinah nor Marijke nor Amsterdam. Drinking and staying drunk was the wisest thing I could think of. I can't remember the taste, only the constant state of randiness. All females on two reasonable legs were welcome to my permanent erection. Drinking did not make me impotent; on the contrary, everything but love seemed irrelevant. The world was on the brink. I hoped to hear the good news of a World War III at any moment, but Truman, alas, prevented MacArthur from throwing the bomb, which would have been a potent solution to all people's troubles and not only mine. I made a bet against myself that if the war in Korea stopped I would change my life and give up alcohol and fornicating, but lost this bet for another five years.

The freedom of the "bohemian" was hell. I depended on others, had to say thank you even if I hated a person's guts. I couldn't accept. Only holy men can accept humbly. Ordinary people like myself were ashamed. My dream of being the doctor to help others remained a dream. I needed help yet did not wish to learn to swim so as not to have to save others from drowning.

I had to make my decision loud and clear, and one evening, while the whole family sat around the baby, I said aloud what everyone knew already: "I am leaving!" Impressed by my own courage, I wanted to dance and sing to a tune that has gone through my head since I saw *It's in the Air* with George Formby back in '39. ("It's in the air . . . tra la la . . . everywhere, that makes me sing without a care—it's in the air.") The ice was broken, the decision made. I left the room for more effect, but as I couldn't stand people talking behind my back for more than a minute, I returned. For the first time since I had known them, the entire family looked cheerful and happy. "When are you leaving?" The old man offered me another three hundred dollars to clear out of town the next day. I accepted and left, to go back to Eylders depressed by their cheerfulness.

And suddenly it was over. I could get out, I could escape,

I could leave a class of people whose mentality I could never digest: The petty-mindedness; the fear of tomorrow; the pursuit of security which is the dream of the nomads; the insult endured which is transported into arrogance and superiority; the martyrdom with which we, an entire lower middle class (Jewish or Gentile), pulled our own cart across the river; the suffering of the people and the ethos which this suffering creates—the cobweb of the endless and senseless torture of always lacking everything, into which we were born. We could never choose our tools for survival; they seemed chosen beyond our concept of choice. We—the lower classes—not distinguished by anything (not even strong fists and pushy shoulders, the endowment of mythical laborers who dream of liberation through physical labor alone), neither strong nor weak, fat nor thin, heavy nor light, highly intelligent nor very stupid, dark nor fair, rich nor poor, specially gifted nor without talent. In other words, a people into which I was born and with whom I have everything in common but my private life and death.

Concerned, I took it with me to Vienna. Leaving Ida was leaving my people—to climb the ladder of my namesake. I felt I owed it to my name to do something more worthwhile with my life than to be the artist manqué, the man who says, "I wanted to do all sorts of things but something or other always prevented me." I had to write it all down. I once tried showing the things I had written to Dr. Hirsch of Fischer Publishing, who at the time lived in Amsterdam. He wisely refused to see me and I thought he had better things to do than look at a private sickness. What I had written was not literature; how could it be? Literature, I believed—together with all the other morons who have a say on what literature is supposed to be—is something aesthetically polished and of general interest, a private life transformed into neatly turned sentences. Literature (the word alone is impressive) is something holy, pure and beautiful. And the low and dirty, the uneducated, the uncouth, the unitiated should not be allowed to enter this Holy of Holies and stand before the God of the Morons. Some of the "morons" were my friends, and some still are to this day. Why not have idiots for friends? Aren't we all made out of the same stuff? I only claim to have been the greatest of them all. Instead of doing "my thing," as they call it, I tried to survive; instead of giving up, I persisted. It's either unloading a car of Vichy water at a railway siding or doing market research. One way or other one could always earn enough to live on, providing one didn't interrupt work with study. Jan Wiegel waited with me for odd jobs at the student labor exchange, and he was a regular student; he had even less time than I, who could come and go as I pleased and was never called to exams. The faculty of politics and sociology had a warm coffee room that was one of its best features.

Occasionally I went and listened to Presser the historian or Klecrekoper the economist, and sometimes I showed up when Barents talked, but usually I fell asleep in the overheated, overfull lecture halls, among students who wrote everything down in notebooks placed on little desks extending from the right arms of their chairs. I don't need to make notes nor do I have to remember anything. No one will ever ask me what the condition of the English miners in the eighteenth century was and no one will ever want to know what Veblen had to say about Malthus. I can't imagine ever coming across anyone who would wish to discuss the effect of Engels' "Anti-

Dühring" on the German working class. I have learned my own theories of politics and history. I have my own ideas about what the German working class said when Engels told them: Dühring is an anti-Semite. They shouted: Work, freedom, bread! The working class is not interested in Jews in particular and vice versa. And what is "economy"? A well-guided economy allows a man to take home sufficient wages to carry on with what he is doing. This "man" usually has a family with a number of children; he works for them. And the children, providing there is cheap medical care, will survive infancy and childhood and create an overpopulation problem that seems solvable only by world wars or black plagues. There is one solution to this problem: education. If a citizen can be taught (slowly and gradually) not to break in, not to murder, which most people don't after all, he can be taught not to make more than two children per couple, so he may enjoy some of the fruit of his labor. Education by fines first (whoever has a third child goes to jail) and those who can't have them get one ready made from the government. But nobody is going to elect me for president so why debate these things theoretically? Because I have to. I'm allowed to unload crates of Vichy water on railroad sidings, sell lottery tickets, collect waste paper, as long as I am registered at the university as a budding intellectual. I hated the intellectual Mafia. What's knowledge good for? To get yourself a job behind a desk so you can keep warm and out of the rain? I could keep warm by sitting in public libraries and reading rooms, coffeehouses and restaurants. I could drink as much as I liked by never missing a party. I could eat whatever there was in the house if I visited either Dinah or Marijke or any other friends. There was always something to eat in someone's home. Why work for it? I worked for train fares

and cigarettes and for my room above a bakery, with a singing woman and her screaming child next door. The room
smelled of sour dough, but one could shut the window. I had
an electric hot plate. I could make tea. I could write whatever came to my mind. I wrote pages and pages, wrote on
every piece of blank paper in sight, and did not think about
Marx and Engels, economics, history and the agricultural
reform in Hungary after Petöfi. Culture and art did not interest me. I wrote because I had nothing to do that was more
fun than writing. I wrote, but didn't read, as I couldn't do
both.

Who is Ulu? Ulu is a young man just returned from Siam.
He collects loafers, students and pretty girls, so he can tell
them all he knows about karma, the Buddha and meditation.
He also uses a tape recorder for sessions of psychodrama.
His second name is Herzberg. Ulu was born in Amsterdam.
How did he get to Siam? Must have hitchhiked there. No,
he arrived via America, he says, after the war. He was a
Dutch refugee child in Milwaukee, poor kid. In Siam he
went into army surplus. Made enough to come back and
now has a good room in town and a tape recorder. He is
rich. He talks good and looks good. Gets all the best-looking
women in town. He is making it. His motive in life: Keep
busy!

. . . and this kind of notes. Occasionally I wrote poems or a
short story; none of them for publication, which is why Amsterdam had been a good place. I could do what I pleased and
no one cared. I was never tired of Dinah and Marijke. Like a
prostitute, I waited for the doorbell to ring, and the ringing
of doorbells has a special meaning for me. When the doorbells rang during the years 1942–45 in Amsterdam, there

was usually a uniformed man who asked you politely to come along and get ready to die.

It was not the German police after all, it was just for a fuck, and that's why I enjoyed it more than I could confess to either Dinah or her friend. I don't get paid for it. I'm doing something good for this town. I was no doubt a godsend fornicating angel who descended on this earth to spread happiness to the many. The depressive and the neurotic were my special charges. I loved them more than good-smelling rich Texas girls—who were apparently out of my orbit. When occasionally I changed this philosophical position and propped myself up at Eylders or took a train to Bussum to talk to my wife and look at my son, it was only to have time to brood over my next move.

The town is small, I know what everyone is doing at any moment of the day and night. It's always the same people, the same girls; that's bad. One more year in this town and I will be a drunken tramp who can't get up from under his newspapers on a bench in Vondel Park; that is bad also. Not enough Vichy water arriving in Amsterdam is good. Let's go on. Dinah is always home, cooks for me and loans me money; that's good. I'm the second man in her life. The first was a Protestant student who thought girls just like to talk; that's bad. I'm no student, I'm a teacher, a professor; that's good. I have finished my study here; that's good. From my modest beginnings in 1943 I have made good progress. I can come twice as often as others, exhaust any woman and still be ready to go to Eylders to find a new one. That's bad; it makes me tired. If I called myself the champion I wouldn't be boasting; it's good but not good enough. It does not pay the rent, so I have to begin to sell myself for money. Impos-

sible, because I'm not "totally indiscriminate" as Ida claims.
I really love Marijke. That she is not rich enough to sup-
port us both I don't hold against her but against myself,
which is my great mistake. More than learning the getting
out of the womb, I have to learn the going back to it before
I can have a chance.

PART TWO

We were either on top of or under the blanket. Off the bed there was nowhere to move but to the stove to put a shovelful of coal into that cold iron. Such quarters are called a *Kabinett,* a cabin. My new life was a new woman. This time the mistakes of the past must not be repeated. The situation had changed; I earned my living, though the way I earned this living was a little peculiar. There was something obscene and not quite moral about it, yet everyone I knew envied me for the job. It took endless weeks of waiting before I was called for a physical checkup. First they checked me under my balls and then under my armpits. All the time they made notes. The police doctor and his female assistant. Finally they asked me: What religion? And when I said, "None," they wrote down RC because in Austria a civil servant is supposed to be of the same confession as the citizens whose servant he is. Even Lutherans or Jews who wanted to work for the censors were expected at least not to object to having RC put after their names. "Only a formality," said the assistant. A strange formality, as the four Allies, our employers, were not; not with names like Garfunkel, Greenfeld, Pomeranz and

Goldschmidt. True enough, the only Austrian they talked to was called Julius Blau, and he was a convert, head of the staff, and more Roman Catholic than the clergy, people said. The pay was reasonable, and the work soft. A pair of scissors and good eyesight was all one needed, and of course a few languages. I knew German, Dutch, French, English, Hebrew, Yiddish—maybe not enough to conduct a sensible conversation, let's say in French, but enough for the Allied Censorship. Enough German to know if a Nazi from Buenos Aires sends another Nazi in Ottakring his kind regards or a visa; enough English to make out whether a man in New York sent his friend twelve diamonds in the brassiere of his mother or will meet him at twelve somewhere at a brasserie. A detailed description of a penis in Hebrew (from a soldier on leave) could not confound me and in Dutch I was perfect—alas, no one ever wrote in this language. We had to report on special preprinted forms everything that concerned political propaganda or black market deals. The politics were only partly of interest, as in this letter from Cairo:

The Jews are back in Austria, but we will return one day and put all the heads of all the yids into a gas chamber until they are blue in their faces—how about that, Rudi? Heil Hitler. P.S. Oh, my sweet Rudi, wouldn't I much rather, like in the good old days, tie you up and whip the "clap" out of you—instead of sitting here in this rat hole Cairo where I have to lick the ass of every former officer cadet just to keep alive?

I was much more interested in the "human story"—in the private sex life, for instance, of a man from Montevideo who recommended to his fiancée in Vienna a dildo made of buffalo hide, oiled with sesame oil, and spiced with ginger for taste. Sworn to secrecy, I could not even tell Dinah what it said in a letter from Beirut:

"Dear Mausi, You wouldn't believe it, but the cunt of your sister, which I thought little, is enormous, and you never told me that. Why didn't you? I closed my eyes for a moment, dreamed I was on a ride through your forest in search of my . . ." This was a love letter only censors get to read and are not allowed to divulge. We sat at the pulse of the occupation and knew what was going on in the world, Bernie Kantorovicz, Avi Eisen and me—all three of us exiled from Israel. Avi thought I could earn more if I helped him sell nylons to the female censors. I knew him from Kibbutz Athlith back in '46, when I worked on a fishing boat and we fished out of Haifa Bay sardines in tins that British customs had dumped for evasion of import duties. Avi wore dark glasses, had regular features and was Viennese; he was pedantic and oversexed, in constant trouble with women. In Athlith he had none, in Vienna too many. Trudi, a big fat blonde, wanted to marry him, as she was pregnant. He had bad memories when threatened in the Viennese dialect (a language which sounds dangerous and really is); he was about to give in but left the ultimate decision to me. In the meantime he had to save up. I suggested that he go to Amsterdam, but he said he could not move because he lived with his parents, a working-class family who had adopted him at birth and shipped him to Palestine in '38, as "I looked Jewish even as a child." To have looked Jewish "even as a child" was one of Avi's troubles. "I never had peace in my life; they always recognized me" sounded like the lament of a leper. In Athlith, Avi's return to the twenty-first district of Vienna, Florisdorf, had been our sole topic of conversation. "Florisdorf is my fatherland. I can only speak Viennese." His versatility in seven languages—English, French, Hebrew, Spanish, Arabic, Italian and Swedish—earned him a bonus

61

from the censors. In Athlith he repaired shoes, which was as luxurious a profession as being a censor in Vienna. "All you do is take a pair of good scissors, put on your glasses, read a few letters, and that's it."

"How is the woman situation?"

"All girls now want only Jews. Did you know that?"

"In Vienna too?"

"It's the same everywhere. They say even in Moscow!"

"Even in Peking?"

"Even in Peking. All non-Jewish girls dream of virile Jewish men like myself. I wonder why—but I don't ask questions. There is something in a circumcised erection that reminds them of a woman's clitoris, and of course women really prefer women, my girl says."

An interesting theory. I tried to discuss it with Dinah, but she didn't like my friends. With her background she had never seen bums like Avi and Bernie. She was brought up on Bach and poetry. She didn't understand that I liked tramps, oddballs, strange creeps and weird maniacs. This trial period for which she had come over could not last through the summer; better to enjoy it while it lasted. I loved her, as I could not but love a Jewish princess. To go anywhere with her was to attract attention among my friends; the presence of a beautiful woman can save a lot of unnecessary talk.

My second friend, Bernard Kantorovicz, had disappeared with the cashbox of the Haifa branch of the Communist party of Palestine and couldn't go back even if he wanted to. Either the police or the party would get him. He had to stay, but hated the Viennese; that's why he had special homework. His line was a bimonthly anticommunist pamphlet sponsored by kind people in Washington, D.C., and he was against Avi's nylons and ballpoints. Bernie hated "business" because he was an intellectual (he said). Avi bought the nylons at the Mandel from a Hungarian but not from my Grünbaum. He knew "Grünbaum, the crook!" If I had to choose a sideline I would have preferred even nylons and ballpoints from Grünbaum to working for the CIA. To my mind communists had been the real anti-Nazis; they had been Hitler's archenemies as much as the Jews. Jews died; the communists, as non-Jews, had a choice but fought them and lost millions of people; that's a fact. Were the Russians not the first to recognize Israel in 1948? Had the Czechs and Poles not helped us with arms, ammunition and planes in the War of Independence? How could one possibly be anticommunist? I was in the position of moralist and Bernie the right man for me to lecture when I wanted to sit up all night. He was an argumentative, loud-mouthed, all-knowing egomaniac, like so many of my friends, and I liked him also because Dinah disapproved, partly because she was jealous (our "political talk" isolated her). Even if she had understood Viennese (she knew only a bad school German) she wouldn't have appreciated the finer points of our strange language. As an ex-communist, Bernie only knew how to use communist clichés to argue against them. His standard phrase was: "Communism, like Nazism, is a recipe for the tyranny and exploitation of the working classes." I translated it for Dinah but it made no sense. I had to translate sentences for her from the writings of communist renegades (as Bernie was proud to call himself) from Koestler to Silone. I was used to disliking my friends and disagreeing with them. I had talked to Nazis during the war; I certainly could talk to Bernie. He was an excellent demagogue who had stories more exciting than the sexual theories of Avi. Avi lived in the Russian sector, Bernie in the American. Being for either one or the other paid off. It was a strange period.

Most Jewish ex-concentration camp inmates (liberated by the Red Army) hated the communists like the bubonic plague, while émigrés back from New York, London, Zurich, Tel Aviv joined the Austrian Communist party. I was a silent admirer of Joseph Stalin—without Stalin's mad, ruthless iron fist the Nazis would never have been smashed by the anarchistic, religious Russians; even today I think this is true—but I didn't care much for the party. On the other hand, I liked Russians, for whom I had an emotional affinity. My real interest has never been politics. I liked "discussions" for the sake of argument. If anyone talked for Stalin, I had a few arguments against him. Fanaticism for any movement, party or ideology seemed to me a loss of personal identity. How can anyone who talks in the plural ever be right?

Dinah left for Amsterdam and promised to return. I waited for her in the Artclub. There had been three places in Amsterdam: Reinders, Eylders and the Kring. In Vienna there was only one, the Artclub, a small unventilated basement off the Kärntnerstrasse, where everyone who did not wish to go home at night could wait until 8 A.M. Qualtinger, Hundertwasser, Fuchs, Artmann, Lehmden, Hutter, Bayer, Friedrich Gulda, George London, Wally. Wally had just arrived from Australia and was definitely the first hippie Europe had seen. She wore torn blue jeans, all-white makeup, black-circled eyes, and she danced and sang to herself. Outside this asylum the Viennese were as grumpy, fat, rude and sleepy as before the war; without a place to drink oneself sick and share the women, it would have been hell. Without an Artclub one would have to pay the Rosis and Mitzis on the Praterstrasse fifty schillings for five minutes while they looked at their wristwatches.

"Hello, Bubi. Want to put it in for a little while?"

"How much?"

"Fifty, room extra."

"That's a lot of money."

"Buzz off then."

Under the railway bridge, a little farther down the Praterstrasse, the price was lower and the work done by hand.

"How much?"

"Ten schillings. But no touching. Please hurry up. Someone is coming. Quick. Here you are! Look at that! Very nice! Like the fire brigade! Watch my dress, you clod! *Servus! Auf Wiedersehen!*"

Dinah returned with a promise from her mother to send us an occasional food parcel. The parcels arrived with Dutch cheese, butter, jam and sausage. Dinah looked after children in an Orthodox Jewish kindergarten on the fifth floor of an old house near the Stephansdom, headquarters of the Agudath Israel party. It didn't pay much but the work was reasonable; all she had to do was play with children, which she liked. The censors were about to close down; my source of information about what was going on in the world was drying up. A letter to a woman named Wilhelmina Pustinger from a woman named Emma Pustinger, postmarked 11/10/51 in Montreal, was my last literary "document":

Darling,

You will be seventy-two tomorrow, but you are still my little girl. If you were here with me I would take you on my lap and tickle you as I did when you were a little girl. Happy birthday!

As always, your loving mother,
Emma

P.S. Your Uncle Adolf died. He was such a nice man, God bless his soul. Alas, he left us nothing, the old fart.

Then the censors ceased operation and I tried to look around for a "future." I decided now seriously to do something more interesting with my time and decided to become a stage director. The work of the actor had always struck me as comparatively easy, requiring mainly a good memory. The work of the director seemed even more attractive. All you have to do is stand or sit around and tell others where they go wrong (instead of from left to right, from right to left). If anyone forgets his lines the director prods an individual called a prompter, who sticks his head out of the orchestra and supplies them. I liked the idea of this kind of job. It seemed easy enough to check where others went wrong. I applied, took my exam and was accepted at the Academy, and once accepted by such a high institute of learning, I convinced the Council and the Joint Distribution Committee to pay me twenty-five dollars a month, the minimum scholarship available for students of drama. I made a "very good" on my entrance exam by indicating stage directions for *Death of a Salesman*, by Arthur Miller, the best modern play around at the time, and registered again as an "extraordinary" student. Why not ordinary? Because I had no diploma to prove that I had ever studied algebra, Latin and trigonometry. I might rise to "ordinary student" by next autumn providing my "progress" in the spring as extraordinary student warranted such promotion.

"What are you doing?"

"Max Reinhardt seminar." Magic words. Friends became distinctly more polite; only delicatessen owners and landladies were not impressed enough. Every second day of the month I got five hundred schillings and this was certainly better than working for the censors from nine to six, five days

66

a week, and getting one thousand schillings a month. For no work, half the pay seemed reasonable progress. I'd be a stage director rather than a censor any time, because while a censor can get bored with what he reads, a stage director can never be bored, as there are always people he has to remind of forgotten lines and wrong steps.

Life changed. I was a student of drama! My life was no longer dramatic—every general of the peasant war, I learned, had a more exciting life than I. That I couldn't pay for my rent, gas, electricity, telephone, food was no tragedy, while the death of one single American salesman was. That's the theater. It turns one's private afflictions, compared with what happened to King Lear when his three daughters left him out in the cold, to something prosaic and profane. Only an actor or a director understands this. Audiences had better look, listen and learn.

It was doubtless because I couldn't understand how I ever got into this marvelous club that I lost my memory and could not memorize more than two lines at a time of any dialogue. Instead of thinking about how to liberate people from oppression, the Duke of Egmont in me thought of how to get out of the flat in the Hauffgasse without paying back rent. It was getting too small for the two of us. We needed a room that was larger and a little nearer the Academy in Hietzing. My teacher didn't care whether I was gradually falling out of love with Dinah. Fred Liewehr, who played all the lovers in town, wanted me to slap my knees and break out in hysterical laughter as Zwirn is supposed to do in Nestroy's *Lumpazivagabundus* when he says: "I told your excellency my daughter is a little backward!" But how to laugh? I couldn't. It was impossible and ridiculous for me to laugh

67

like Zwirn. I had nothing to laugh about. Dinah, fed up with living with a poor student who ran away from her, cried, and at school I was supposed to laugh between eleven and twelve o'clock!

It was all right for Nicole Heesters, whose father was a musical star, the Rex Harrison of all German musicals, or Maria Emo: her daddy was a film producer, in the process of remaking all the prewar Viennese schmaltz with chambermaids, officers, roguish lovers and heartbroken mothers. The Academy was fine for all those who could go home and say, "I need a bit more pocket money." I laughed only on every second day of the month and smiled for six or eight days afterward. The rest of the month I had to avoid creditors and look serious, if not because of Dinah, then because of the serious impression I had to make.

"You owe us eight hundred and fifty schillings!"

"Eight hundred and fifty schillings?"

"If you don't pay tomorrow there will be no more credit."

"I will pay tomorrow, I promise."

In my family debts were considered shameful; that's why I had to promise to pay. The next day I went to shop somewhere else, paid the first few days with borrowed money and then let them chalk it up. Once the debt exceeded my capital I moved on to the next store for new credit, et cetera. Dinah, not used to real life, looked worried and waited for the police to come and put me in jail.

"They didn't get me during the war; who will arrest me now?"

"The war is over. You have to pay your debts."

"Who says so?"

"You have to. You can't go on like this!"

"Why not? I'm not stealing. I'm just short of cash. When I have it I'll pay them back."

Which was true. Somehow I always managed to cover previous debts.

"It makes me nervous. Your way of life makes me sick."

"I like it. It isn't ideal but it's better than working for the censors. I'm now a student. One day I'll earn money."

"I don't believe it."

I didn't believe it either; I too was convinced it could not go on forever, but we had to eat. As an extraordinary student of war I knew exactly what to do in wartime; for peacetime existence I had no training. If once I had been of the bourgeosie—as I had considered myself for years—I now seemed like an anarchist compared to Dinah. She never learned to dance on a rope. She had survived in hiding while I survived by thinking quick and walking in the open. She had kept a pure soul, while I had sullied mine with the wish to be alive when everything was over. Yet I decided we should stay together, at least for the time being. How could I possibly leave an elegant, beautiful, long-legged, for me even rich Jewish princess who was naïve and innocent enough to be shocked by my way of life?

All school is hard; this one was even hard to get to, without the fare for bus or streetcar. For a few stops I could always hide behind the backs of fat people; the rest I had to walk. This was a school that would teach me to laugh when I wanted to howl—a school to make a bum into a realistic citizen of this world.

To feel . . . I didn't like this verb; I didn't like the idea; I didn't like the reference. Feel it! I feel it. Can you feel it? What do you feel? Does it feel nice? Do you like the feeling?

Feel, don't think! I liked to think about *it*, not "feelings"—
or rather I didn't, when I felt something, like to like feelings.
I felt limp. My right side ached as if a bone had been removed
and not replaced. With one woman I felt complete. Two people are a powerful presence—a right partner is added
strength, to both woman and man. I sincerely believed that
only the two that make one are a perfect human being. The
real problem was a philosophical one. How can one be complete and do something of interest if one has a permanent
erection? Unthinkable, because the best part is the erection;
as soon as you are rid of it you must get up and work. Therefore it is wanting the erection and not losing it by fucking one
must strive after. In order to have peace and erection one
has to have one right woman only, for life; best for this
purpose is a loving and understanding sister and friend, which
of course has the considerable disadvantage of being less
exciting. It is one woman for one man for a man who loves
his work and wants to keep his erection. To waste it on a
great variety of not sisterly and not friendly but stimulating
females and yet to keep it, is a philosophical problem—and
certainly not a matter of feelings. It was hard enough to keep
us excited without more feelings than it needed to play
demented father and lesbian daughter, grandmother and
aged sister, first cousins at the age of twelve, two strangers
in a country jail, two lesbians in a car, and games of that
kind.

The sex revolution was a private decision, a hobby of every
man born between the Urals and the English Channel. We
needed no revolution, just a supply of Ernas. Politics, story-
telling, yes, but no conversation without exchanging the latest
news on who with whom, how often, when and where; these

70

were problems of great and strategic importance. After all, we were not sissies, Anglo-Saxon students, Jewish Catholic Protestant hypocrites. We were real tantric mystic eastern devotees.

BERNIE: Did you see me the other night with the dark-haired girl with glasses? What did you think of her?

ME: She seems all right.

BERNIE: Seems all right? You ignorant ass. Want to know a secret?

ME: Yes. Let's have it.

BERNIE: She is not just all right. She is ideal.

ME: You said the same thing about Lotte. Ideal! (*Spits on the floor.*)

BERNIE (*looking at me with hand shading his eyes*): You ignorant idiot, you fool. This one is not just a fuck. I say ideal. (*Lifts his voice.*) Incredible! Superior! There is no other one like her (*paces up and down*) here in this goddamned town. Inge, Lotte, Bertha and Trudi (*lowers his voice*)—we know them all and fucked them all—are lousy (*shouts suddenly and with increasing crescendo*) amateurs compared to Herta. (*Softly.*) This one is a professional man-killer who can kill us all. (*Nervous.*) She has the most fantastic body. Her breasts are neither too small nor too big, neither hanging down too much nor rising too high—too high breasts can be a nuisance. I once knew a girl called Veronica whose nipples reached practically to her neck and I couldn't get them between my fingers when I sucked her cunt. (*Sits down and looks at me, breathes twice deeply.*) Herta is married, my friend. (*Head shaking.*) What a shame! She is the greatest woman the world has ever seen! (*Pause. As I*

71

said nothing, he continued—it was his evening.) Incidentally, how do you feel on top of a woman?

ME: On top of a woman, Bernie, I'm out of myself. On top of a woman I think I'm somewhere else, reading a book, writing a letter or doing something relaxing.

BERNIE: I see what you mean. I feel the same.

Never to be tired of explaining, describing, painting exact detailed pictures of what happened, how and how often, and with whom, had its own poetry. The final sentence in a lengthy description of a fantastic orgy, invented or real, was invariably: "What's sex all about? What is this fucking after all? Shit! In and out, in and out, out and in. Fooey! All holes have their limits! It's a tragedy! A misunderstanding, all of it. From ten to twenty masturbate; from twenty to forty fornicate; after forty contemplate." That was Bernie's best advice on the subject. I was only twenty-five. In the middle of it.

"How about an old and ugly woman of eighty-eight, Bernie?"

"Even an old and ugly woman of eighty-eight is a woman. A woman is a woman. Who am I to think one is better than another? What arrogance! All women are beautiful!"

"Would you fuck a lame old crippled woman of eighty-eight?"

"Delighted, and it would be good for both of us. She would think she is still alive and make me feel generous and virtuous, practically a saint."

The subject was inexhaustible, as everyone I knew had an opinion or an experience worth talking about. Wolfgang Pechler, a shy horn-rimmed student of theatrical design, tried to sum it all up:

"Only the rich are beautiful; all other women are ugly. If you make it with a rich woman you are not losing good sperm. If you lay just any girl you are an idiot, a wastrel. You should be locked up!"

But I thought neither Pechler nor Bernie had the ultimate answer. That came from my high priestess, Erna: "The essence of real life consists in experiencing love, in body and mind, as a superior pleasure with the world."

Before the Anschluss he had been personal assistant to Max Reinhardt, but shortly afterward, in December '38, he organized the anti-Semitic exhibition "Jews Look at You" in the same building, featuring Max Reinhardt the Jew and his destructive decadent Jewish teachings. Everybody in town knew that. When Niederführ, in the meantime elevated to school headmaster, met me in the corridor and we seemed to be alone, we had a little very-private talk. "It's not because you are a Jew, Mr. L., that I can't give you the part of Othello. You are just not ready for it. I hope you understand." "Yes, sir." I don't know what made him think in the first place that I thought he wouldn't let me have the part of Othello because I was a Jew. I never thought I should be either an Othello or a Hamlet, a Lear or a Faust, though I wouldn't have minded being a Cyrano de Bergerac, for which I thought my nose would be the right length. I hadn't a chance, Jew or not: I wouldn't have remembered lines even if I had converted.

Herr Professor Neugebauer—he had sad eyes and I liked him for it—didn't mind. He usually wore his herringbone coat with the brown fur collar and his green Austrian hat in class (because the heating was bad) and he never apologized for not giving me the biggest part in a play. "I believe"—he put it more diplomatically—"you actually registered to study *régisseur*. You don't need to do all this; yet, of course, a director who has been an actor has a better understanding of the actor's problems." My understanding of actors' and directors' problems exceeded all documented knowledge in this field. But how to make this clear? "I am probably a future playwright, Herr Professor. My troubles will always be my own." I wasn't even quite sure whether theater was the real thing, after all, for me; certainly not this kind of theater, where we played an unfailing, repetitive repertoire of bores. Except Molière and Chekhov—and occasionally Shakespeare. I liked Chekhov, but wished they'd teach us Russian to act him in the original. My real trouble was with the German language. I couldn't stand the sound of German attempting to convey a Russian kind of wry humor and introspective sadness, and maybe it was only because of the German language that I didn't appreciate Ibsen or Strindberg and disliked Anouilh and Giraudoux, while Goethe and Schiller and the entire German repertoire, which also included Kleist and Lessing, seemed definitely beyond my comprehension. The German language had dried up on me; all there was left of it was a crust of standard phrases. Trying to recite the words of the great poets—heroes of my early childhood—was more an exercise in psychodrama, and I kept saying English swear words between sentences of Goethe to feel better, because occasionally I too rattled off in front of the class my version of "To be or not to be."

Language affected my love for Erna and Dinah and my work at the Academy. I couldn't really talk to Dinah; we didn't seem to speak the same language, though I can speak Dutch. I couldn't talk to Erna because her lessons were silent, nor could I like the language of German drama or translated comedy. My sense of humor in the German language had left me since I had heard it used to yell and scream at people with venom and hatred, with threats and murderous slogans, since it became a language of decrees and curfews, inhuman laws and black-framed announcements, a language of lies and falsehood, of murder and death. German had been till then my private oasis to hide from this world, the only safe place I could retreat to when the world around had gone insane.

On a day in March '38 this well of my privacy in the universe was destroyed forever by the millions of people who later drowned in a Teutonic abyss of *Achtung*s and *Wird erschossen*s, which followed the *Judenraus* and *Judasverrecke* language. Now German gave me the creeps and there was no use in arguing this. "What has this got to do with Bertolt Brecht or Heinrich von Kleist? What has it to do with my German friends who write books in German?" Nothing; it had nothing to do with the people who wrote and write it—as it wasn't what they *said*, but that they said it *in German,* that disturbed me more than I cared to admit to anyone. When I talked about it, my friends either shook their heads feeling sorry for me, believing I had spent my years in Buchenwald or Auschwitz, or simply called me neurotic, hypersensitive, mad—and maybe I really had lost my sense of reality, and the German language had not been affected by the Nazis, only my feelings had. Madder than anything was to think I could ever unlearn sounds I knew by heart and kidneys and replace them with other and better sounds. To do that, I had to try to go back to a time before I knew any language, back into a near autistic state of mind that communicates on a level of la-la. In order not to get too deep into these diapers (and I was conscious it was regression), I had to switch my concern from basic needs for food and shelter—the political-economic bag—to a universal, essential state of existence that begins even before speech, before hearing. I had to replace the private with the universal, which in practice meant I existed in a permanent state of mess and disorder, in a primordial chaos, without the ordering soothing creative energy of words. I had to learn to make my own private language, which I then could apply in any tongue. I had to discover my own references to things, people and ideas, which I would afterward be able to express in any language, even Chinese and Swahili. My Chinese and Swahili was English. I didn't have the patience to study the books one could borrow from the English or American reading rooms. My English teachers were my friends David Bronson and Mike Mabry. Anyone who spoke English as his mother tongue was automatically a friend, as if I myself had come from across the sea, like them, to study. But I wasn't really one of them; only in my mind. After all, I was born in Vienna and therefore at home here. Did I or did I not belong to them? As long as I cared about "in" and "out," I was "out." Americans and English clamor to be loved by the rest of the world, instead of just taking it for granted. In spite of the fact that they fought Hitler and the Japanese and won, they feel guilty. To my English and American friends, who hardly knew where Europe was and knew nothing of what war was until they came here, I was just another "Continental" student of their language. The difference between a social democrat, a right-wing conservative, an anti-Semitic monarchist, a communist Austrian and a Jew from Budapest I had to teach them. Neither David nor Mike knew that:

1. a Hungarian baron was usually a Jewish industrialist who received a knighthood under Emperor Franz Josef II;

2. a *Gaskammertachenierer* was a Jew too lazy to lift his legs to go to the gas chamber;

76

3. Kravots and Bems (Croats and Czechs) were foreigners who didn't know English.

Our differences were not languages but incomes.

The scheme was cooked up by a small, wiry Bulgarian with a black mustache who operated from his private apartment overlooking the Danube canal. He had forty or fifty students on the road, traveling up and down the country with sample pages of what the "Who's Who" was going to look like.

Anton Widerhöfer
Born 10 July 1880 in Kirchleiten
Married, 2 sons, 1 daughter
Made assistant in 1901 and master in 1914
Served with the II K & K infantry regiment in
    Penzgau (1916–18)
Awarded Iron Cross, third class
Mayor of Pschörr two terms, 1927 and 1928
Owner of the smithy The Golden Horseshoe
    in Niederbrunn

was a typical sample page.

For the privilege of getting into this "Austrian Artisans' Who's Who," the shoemakers, carpenters, blacksmiths, wheel and barrel makers, bakers, butchers and tailors had to pay four hundred schillings—half of it down, half fourteen days before publication date. In the price was included a "Certificate signed and sealed" by the Secretary of the Guild and the President of the Chamber of Commerce of the county, and all this came printed in large black gothic letters, framed with gilded flower petals and ready to be put under glass and fastened to the wall to be admired by friends and members of the family forever after. "What more can I give you for a lousy four hundred schillings?" said the Bulgarian. We got forty percent not only of the down payment (this wouldn't have been a good deal) but of the total, which meant that the Bulgarian made 240 to our 160 schillings. Once the artisans had signed the contract they were pressured and threatened from his office until they settled the second half of their debt as promised two weeks before publication of the "Who's Who" (which of course never appeared). In four weeks' walking and hitchhiking around villages near the Czech border, a part of the world further removed from civilization than the middle of Brazil, I made four thousand schillings and felt rich enough to pack up the job, pay some of my debts and move to a "very fine" room in a large apartment.

Mrs. Scholz was a stately woman with glandular trouble. Her blue eyes pressed against her thick glasses when she was angry and her neck seemed stuffed with bread and onions. She lived with her two Pekingese dogs, Pik and Pok, on restitution moneys—her (Jewish) husband had died just at the beginning of '38, but who would find out?—and on subletting her rooms. Like no one else, she knew who was who in our street. "Don't go to the beer house on the corner; the owner is an old SA man. He looted all the Jewish homes in the street—that's how he became rich." Mr. Breitschneider, who owned the beer house on the corner, was small fry. Former Gestapo men and officers of the SS were elected mayors of small towns and sat in high positions in government and industry, or were pensioned off with full salaries to the end of their lives. Mrs. Scholz blamed the Allies. "They should do something, do something!" My new landlady was a pathetic, lonely Viennese woman. Her other tenants were David Perlman and Therese. David's job was to talk to Zurich, to see how his dollars and Swiss francs were doing, from bed. Therese, a simple, plain-

78

looking girl from Mattersburg in Burgenland, washed and mended his socks and underwear, cooked his goulash with dumplings and amused him in bed. "She pays me restitution— her share in the collective guilt. Every time I see her wash my underwear and iron my shirts, I know she feels I have forgiven them everything they did to us. I just can't hit her. She asks me to hit her, the bitch, but I have a soft heart." When Therese needed money to do shopping for both of them and wanted to buy herself a new pair of stockings, she first had to promise to repay every penny "as soon as possible" by going out to work.

"Aren't you ashamed to be a Jew, Mr. L.?" Mrs. Scholz asked me because of David's treatment of Therese.

"No, Mrs. Scholz. Jews are just like other people, apart from being different. We have our bastards and crooks, swindlers, robbers and even fascists. What arrogance to think we must be better just because we are different."

Certainly not all of us. Maybe we should, but who should not be better? Personally I couldn't have cared less whether David was Jewish or aboriginal; I pitied his dumb girl friend from Mattersburg, wished her a better man and was drawn back into an orbit I thought I'd left by quitting Amsterdam. But ultimately it was the material, not the Jewish, question I had to solve.

I registered at the student labor exchange, where two pimply Catholic female students had the latest information. "They need one more student in a warehouse in Hütteldorf."

"How much do they pay?"

"Fifty schillings a day and overtime."

"What's the work?"

"Rolling barrels."

"What kind of barrels?"

"Barrels with lard or sauerkraut."

Who would believe people can eat so much sauerkraut? Barrels rolled down the yard as if fired from a gun. The trucks dumped them at the entrance, we shot them into the basement and stacked them three or four high. Work in the courtyard was easy and pleasant, in the cold and damp catacombs not so good. To stack the first row was easy enough, the second harder, the third quite difficult. The ceiling permitted a fourth layer in the midship cellar and this could be dangerous work. Occasionally I had to jump for my life.

"He was killed by a barrel of sauerkraut."

"I don't believe it. He just doesn't want to come home. I know him."

Once a barrel is on its path it keeps on rolling. If it hadn't been so far away from town—half an hour by train—if the pay had been a little better and the stench in the basement less, I might have stayed until fired. After a week I sold my job to a Rumanian, who sold it to a fellow Rumanian for a bottle of vodka. ("What do you expect—a Rumanian!") Why did people hate the Rumanians? Everyone called them thieves, swindlers, cheats. "Because the saying 'A Rumanian is a *ganef*' was not invented by us, but by the Visigoths," according to Bernie. "That's why." The Rumanian I sold my job to dealt in guts for sausages on Saturdays and Mondays only. He bought them by weight and sold them by length. A friend of his imported the guts from Rumania ("Twenty kilos of guts is a small fortune!" he lectured me) and he offered me a job helping him, collecting the suitcases they arrived in, usually ten at a time, from the railway station. Duty had to be paid on the guts, but by knowing the right people at the station, even after everyone had been paid off there was money in it.

"What do you do with all the guts?"

"Sausages, my friend; everybody eats sausages. Sausages are the answer to all the world's problems. You eat a good sausage and you know you can cope with anything." I liked the Rumanian—I liked all Rumanians—and would have worked for him for fun, but the pay he offered was so-so and the job questionable. "When everyone involved in a guts deal is Rumanian, don't touch it," was another saying of Bernie's. My only chance was to go back to study—neither the "Who's Who" nor the sauerkraut could get me out of this mess. I owed Mrs. Scholz two months' rent and neither Dinah nor Erna nor anyone else could help me here. I had to become a theater director for lack of an alternative.

It was not that easy. Any systematic study was out of the question. I couldn't listen. Learned talks always bored me, even on "interesting" topics. Nor could I read a book discussing art, the theater, dramatic literature, architecture. It was hard enough to read plays. To avoid dropping out at some later stage in life, I tried not to get "in" to start with. I liked the ordinary things—eating, drinking, sleeping and a lot of fornicating. Art, culture, literature or anything loosely connected with loads on the mind I detested, but as I had to do something, I ultimately loved the Academy I was about to leave after one year. Even if I didn't learn to speak any other man's lines, I listened to them. I learned to shut up my own sound, and to suppress even the suggestion of having my own voice as too much trouble. In the solving of the material question (to quote Gurdjieff) was the solution of everything. Because life consists in living and paying for it.

My eventually leaving this town and this school was engendered by another of those coincidental encounters one sees in perspective only much later. *Die Heimkehr* ("The Road Back") was a trashy story about a Jewish refugee professor who comes back to Germany and his university and is driven out of his job by a gang of anti-Semitic students. The leader of these young Nazis turns out to be (who wouldn't have guessed?) Siegfried, his very own son, whom he had to leave behind in '35 when he emigrated. Kortner, short, stocky and stern, like a small inquisitor in a gray suit and striped tie, introduced his movie, played the main role and addressed the students afterward, looking for more Siegfrieds as he stood there, hands on his hips, an inquisitor of the Jews speaking in traditional German-professor tones. The students repeated more or less, but less noisily than the students in the movie, that whatever a returned Jewish professor had to say on this subject must be exaggerated. In the opinion of all my classmates, Jews who had returned from America came back to rub every German's and Austrian's nose into the shit of his own past, making the big mistake of believing that Austrians and Germans were as superhuman as they were and should only feel sorry for the Jews! What about their own sufferings under Hitler? They too had to survive bombardments at home, the shortages of food and heat, the artillery of the Russians, the looting and raping afterward and the de-Nazification courts of the Allies in the immediate postwar years of hunger and cold —while the emigrants waited in New York and Hollywood until Austria and Germany, more or less rebuilt, invited them to come back. Kortner looked around for support of his view that the Jews were innocent and their fate incomparable, and got none. He needed aid from some quarter. I thought it was over but there it started again—instead of choosing the side of the many I chose the side of the Jew. Kortner, of all people, turned me back into a Jew. "I believe you, Mr. Kortner," I said. "If they hate us because we remind them of their past, then we shouldn't be here. We must go." Kortner was shocked at converting only a single fellow Jew to his message, and it was at that moment I realized I had to leave Vienna. (Kortner, God bless his soul, of course stayed in Munich, as it was apparently not as dangerous as he thought.) Once I had sided with the Allies and emigrants openly and had made it clear to others that I didn't feel I belonged here, it was time to quit. The war had nothing to do with them, it was our problem, not theirs, if we decided to live here. I should have left school the day after the incident with Kortner, as I had taken on the role of martyr and ex-concentration camp inmate publicly and ostracized myself. I went to great lengths to tell everyone who wanted to listen that I personally had never been arrested or physically molested by either Germans, Austrians or Nazis. "So why did you back that old fart?"

"As a matter of principle, or maybe to annoy you all. Identification with victims is not necessarily the result of a personal experience. Siding with the communist and Jewish victims of fascism is a matter of principle." I held many discussions on this principle, and became as isolated as a crank or an eccentric. It wasn't my full-time job to chase ex-Nazis (as Simon Wiesenthal did); I had to make sure I could go on existing.

Jungles of pubic hair, mountains and valleys of vaginas and breasts were not the real landscape either. Erna had given me all the lessons in love I could take. I knew France as only a few war-torn towns seen through a train window. France and the French I associated with art and literature, and those with

listening to esoteric "in" talk. France was for me a hypo-
chondriacal flavor of "beautiful words" written by men named
Sartre, Gide, Baudelaire and Cocteau. French cultural life
struck me as a kind of Mediterranean fish market, where a
lot seemed to be going on but nothing ever happened, not since
Beckett, and Beckett is not French. Probably because I went
broke in Paris I didn't like the French. They built a huge
monument at the Invalides for the greatest European butcher
preceding Adolf Hitler, then proceeded to live well, eating
and drinking like peasants in their most expensive saloons.
Yet a country as Cézanne, Renoir, Van Gogh, Monet portrayed
it couldn't be all that bad. Of the English I knew even less.
I had seen or heard of them as policemen in Palestine, had
met a few officials and students, and had looked at books and
posters in the English reading room. It looked a dull, chilly,
stiff, monarchistic, pompous life to me, a mixture of smug
suburbia and elegant colonialism—which it was in the early
'50s. No France. No England. Of Italy all I knew was what
I had seen passing my train window between Menton and
Ventimiglia. The sight of widows in black and handsome
young men had made me sad. The Italians I had met on the
train all seemed to be elegant fops, dark-glassed spivs, priests
or shouting policemen. Italian women, I thought, stick to you
like pasta if you make the mistake of hauling them into bed;
that's what I saw in the movies. I liked their picture postcards—landscapes set in a melancholy of Sicilian songs. Of
Belgium I remembered black marketeers and very fat whores
with bad teeth from the war.

The sadness, the boredom, the nausea was everywhere, in
everyone. The world outside was locked away behind borders,
visas, permissions, checkbooks, identity cards and labor per-
mits. Vienna was obviously the only place in the world I

could live in and I'd better like it, whether I like it or not. Voluntarily or not, I began to sniff the Viennese air as if it were a padded and soundproof cell in a monastic loony bin, where everyone is ultimately left alone and penniless to ponder his own punishment on the day of judgment.

Vienna, I discovered, was a more mystical city than Jerusalem. A city that elevates material suffering to spiritual revelation is a mystical city. This instruction comes, in cruel eastern fashion, as a realization that in Vienna there is neither hope nor future. The little gold there is is on the leaves in the autumn woods. Vienna teaches you to stay within your dream. Somewhere in the far west, as seen from Vienna, life is a business, if a dreary one, and not just an ornament. Vienna, then, was for the mystic and I didn't wish to turn into a mystic. I wanted to get out of my skin and out of this town, where people believe they think when they sit up all night and talk the pigeons from the roof and are never bored with their introspective twists and turns through the lush thicket of their morbid and oversensualized fantasies. People in Vienna like to talk, not only for the sake of talking but also to watch others talk. They like to watch you talking, not to listen to what you have to say. Every twitch and twinkle, yawn and grin, the stretching and shrinking movements of the face while the words fall out of the mouth, are observed under a microscope. Not even the sound of the mouth matters here; only the face and the eyes.

Dinah's dark, beautiful, sad, reproachful eyes looked at me when I considered leaving her. Should I have settled down in them? I only married to divorce; I liked to be alone, to get ready for the day when I would say all that was on my mind. Not to be too serious about my future as a "professional intellectual" enhanced my pleasure in anything I did. The

85

crazier and the less permanent the better. My only defense against her black eyes, which tried to hypnotize me (I imagined into marriage), was to prove to her and to myself that I was obviously good for nothing.

I certainly was not good enough to do anything more interesting; that's why I went to "collect money" for a photographer named Peter Funk, a big fat slob of a man with a velvet voice and a soft giggle, who was too lazy to climb stairs and ring the doorbells of people who "owed him money," or rather would owe him money if they bought his photographs of their children. Peter photographed schoolchildren one by one during their recess and produced nicely trimmed post-card-size pictures of them, presented in folders, three at a time, for a reasonable price. To convince parents to buy twelve picture postcards required a certain diplomacy, depending on who the parent was. A simple housewife would say, "I never ordered these pictures," but a more sophisticated woman suggested, "How about having supper with us instead of cash?"

A lot of staircases to climb and a lot of stories to listen to before someone dipped into his wallet. "It's better than just collecting money," Peter Funk had lectured me. "All parents are happy to pay for a picture of their child." The few happy hours I had were when I felt a lot of cash in my pocket. My trouble was figuring out the thirty percent. What I called thirty percent and what Peter called thirty percent always differed—to his advantage. He always had a huge grin when I left. I wanted to learn to be clever yet stay a fool.

It didn't last long and was more instructive than working for Funk.

"You going up to Herta?"

"Why?"

"Don't."

"Why not?"

"I'll show you something."

He pulled me over to the window and showed me a black and blue ring around his right eye.

"From a butcher who said I stepped on his heels. The first few days he pretended he had not seen me, but yesterday he suddenly turned around and knocked me into the gutter with a sharp right. Nearly killed me. Just went to see Herta about damages."

"What did she say?"

" 'Clear out.' I'll have the police on her."

Which police? Herta specialized in shadowing people, from butchers to policemen. Her customers were the jealous wives and girl friends who wanted to know everything. "The private eye has to keep at a safe distance from the person he observes, or he might become a suspect and get himself into trouble. Watch your step and all will be well," she lectured me. Herta was an elderly woman with a hairnet and horn-rimmed glasses, a kind of sergeant major in skirts, chewing a pencil instead of a cigar.

"You can start tomorrow."

"What am I supposed to do?"

She went over to a filing cabinet, returned with a passport picture of a pale and fat face in its late forties under a wide-brimmed approximately gray hat with a lighter-colored hatband. "His name is Johan-Baptist Bimmer. He lives at Föhngasse fifteen, just behind Schönbrunn, near the subway station. You take line forty-nine or seventy-two, but they don't run very frequently."

"What do I do when I get there?"

"You keep a little distance from the house. He should leave at eight-thirty A.M. and carry a cello. He walks to the subway station and takes line E at eight forty-six. He gets off at the Concerthaus and disappears through the main entrance. He rehearses from nine-fifteen until one P.M., then he takes line sixty-two in front of the Concerthaus. Don't let him out of sight. See you the next morning at nine. Everything clear?"

"How much?"

"Five schillings an hour and all expenses. Streetcar fares and phone calls not included."

"Can I take a lunch break?"

"You mustn't lose sight of him."

At eight twenty-five I waited. Fifty yards above Föhngasse 15. Nothing. At eight forty-five a pale fat man under a gray hat left number 15 and walked with the self-confidence of a pasha, with a woman on either side but without a cello, to the subway. (He could of course have left it at the rehearsal yesterday; why carry a cello every day?) Without the cello my trail was useless. Yet I had to follow a man who left number 15 at that time of day. I got paid for it, not for standing around. For a change I had an actual, not a philosophical problem. It had to be solved right away. What if it's a fake Bimmer and I miss the true one, who might in the meantime disappear? What does a real detective do in my place? A real detective acts. I went after them. I tried not to walk too fast but eventually had to run to catch up. Walking across the grass is not allowed, nor is pissing behind a bush. A woman watched me and unexpectedly I heard, "Somebody's pissing!" The man who was not Bimmer—I checked this against the picture in my pocket—advised, "Don't look!" I chased back through the gate and up the road, just in time. Nearly missed the real Bimmer, who appeared at nine-thirty (an hour late!), with cello but without women.

This time someone in curlers appeared at a second-floor window and shouted, "Get after him!" I pretended I hadn't seen or heard this. When the train rumbled into the station I jumped into the fifth car, keeping a two-car distance, and as the train was more or less empty I could easily keep an eye on him. From a safe distance I felt sorry for a poor bastard who fiddled his fingers off for an unattractive middle-aged woman. But my sympathy for Bimmer was hard to sustain. Ultimately I was worse off than he. Half a dozen creditors would be happy to know where I hung out and if I left home it was to chase through town like a hare for five schillings an hour, while he could sit down warm and comfortable in the overheated Concerthaus, play the cello and be paid the minimum twenty schillings an hour for cellists and oboists. Bimmer disappeared through the door; Mrs. Herta had predicted correctly. I took up a position on a bench in a small park opposite. I hid behind a newspaper, began to doze off in the sun, and when finally I woke up from my nap the rehearsal was over and some musicians had left. To find out whether my man had gone, I crossed the road and bumped into him. I nearly knocked the cello out of his hand. He turned and gave me a mean look. I decided to leave it at that, walked away and turned around only when he had disappeared, probably on line 62, direction Karlsplatz. Alas, he was gone and could no longer be shadowed, but counting everything, I had still made thirty-five schillings today, which was a more profitable working day than rolling barrels of sauerkraut. I wasn't the first who had lost Bimmer immediately after rehearsal.

"What's the explanation?"

"He was too quick." Mrs. Herta would have to think up a better story to keep her account with the woman in curlers. "He knows he is being followed," I suggested.

"Of course he does; *he* is no fool. As it was your first day, you can try a bit harder tomorrow. Tomorrow is your last chance." A frightening warning.

She went to the filing cabinet and came back with a passport photograph of a man in a police uniform. I refused.

"I run away from cops, Mrs. Herta, I cannot run after them."

"Why? Are you scared?"

"Yes, I'm scared."

"Have you done something to be scared of a policeman?"

"Done? Me? Nothing."

"Well, then, this will teach you to understand that even a policeman is human. Tomorrow at two-thirty P.M., Officer Rudolph Schurz arrives at the Vöslauer Bridge by line number twelve. He usually takes either line forty-one, forty-six or one twelve to Mohrgasse nine and stays until he leaves."

"Yes, Mrs. Herta."

"The time he enters the building doesn't matter. We want to know when he comes out. And you, young man—don't move until he leaves." She flashed her pencil. "After seven P.M. you receive overtime, six schillings per hour instead of five. Report back Saturday morning at nine A.M. sharp and make sure you have something to report."

"What if Mohrgasse nine has a back exit?"

She gave me a filthy look for so much cynicism. I thought she should have been pleased: I obviously intended to take my job seriously. "There is a rear exit, that's true, but at the moment it's closed due to repairs. Anything else?"

"Can I call off the watch at midnight?"

"You can leave when he leaves."

I put Rudolph in my wallet and planned to watch him real carefully all night long, yet keep one eye open for anyone who could let me have one hundred schillings for a few days or could take Rudolph off my hands for half price.

No one wanted the job and no one had one hundred schillings to spare. I had no option. I went to see my police officer next day at 2:30 P.M. at the Vöslauer Bridge. Convinced Rudolph had spotted me as soon as he stepped from line number 12, I did not take the next streetcar with him and arrived at a bar opposite Mohrgasse 9 at 3:30 P.M. Occasionally I went out to look for a cop resembling Officer Rudolph Schurz. After four or five drinks I couldn't tell the difference between one cop and another. I should have gone home right away but was afraid Mrs. Herta might have an inspector trailing me. The streets in this area were deserted at that time of night and all shutters down. I counted the minutes in schillings. Suddenly two cops on their beat stood before me. I hadn't seen them coming.

"What are you doing drunk on a corner at this time of night?"

"I work for the Herta agency"—to my surprise they'd never heard of her—"and it's my job to stay here."

"Beat it."

"It's my job."

"Beat it or we turn you in."

As I had a date at one and had made my one hundred schillings, I left. Mrs. Herta deducted twelve percent from my wages for earning money; twelve percent for a national pension at sixty-five, five percent for my health, three percent for the trade union membership for private eyes, and she refused to pay me for a half-hour tea break.

I thought of contacting Rudolph right away if I could find him to have Mrs. Herta arrested. For the world of a taxpaying citizen I was neither sly nor quick nor diligent enough—and had therefore and obviously no choice but to return to my Academy and try to survive on twenty-five dollars a month. Maybe wrongly, I regarded the Academy as the easiest of all available opportunities.

The disadvantage of being an ordinary registered student was that I had to be there at all lessons and prepare for exams at the end of the term. I specialized in "Silent Scenes by Stanislavsky," taught by Helena Polewitskaya, ex-Moscow Art Theater actress and one of the earlier Ninas in Chekhov's *Seagull,* who left Moscow in 1917. As she was a foreigner here just like myself (thirty-five years in this town hadn't changed that), I liked her, and the sympathy was mutual. Occasionally she even called me her most promising student. Silent Scenes didn't require memorized lines. Quite the contrary, not a word must be spoken. The title, the only thing we were allowed to say, had to sum up what was going on. Silent Scenes were designed to give the actor a chance to learn to feel at least something before he opened his mouth to let out a barrage of words. My best scene was "Love and Career": A woman waits for her man; when he finally returns he looks to the door, expecting someone else to come in. A second man arrives and waits for the first to come along with him. The first man can't make up his mind; torn between his woman and his friend, he sits down to brood over his problem. In the meantime the woman leaves crying, the second man leaves shaking his head and man number one is left alone.

The scenes were always performed in front of the entire class, and as everyone did scenes, no one ever missed the classes of Helena Polewitskaya; besides, she was the kindest and most charming teacher we had at school. Everyone liked this scene from my private life, which more or less depicted what was about to happen in the very near future. Dinah had taken up psychology at the university so as to do something more worthwhile with her time than wait for me to come home, and it was time for me to leave now as well.

I met her at Gerhard's, the composer who threw the wildest parties in town. He had the money for it and the apartment. She wore red ankle socks, sat on a swing and sang. She sang like a cherub, babbled like a child, laughed loud and shrieked and found everything funny. Literally everything was funny for Elizabeth. Life was one big fun fair in which we, the Continentals, walked around like mourners. Her smile did it to me. She looked at me as if I were out of a Glasgow freak show. Until I met her I had thought I was quite funny, but in her eyes I seemed as cheerful as Frankenstein's monster. She imitated everything I said and did, she made fun of me. She wore heavy makeup, which was not customary for girls on the Continent at the time, but later was imitated from imported women's magazines. The English word *makeup* is untranslatable and in fact has never been translated. The effect of her makeup was very powerful. She laughed all the time, but how could I know if she was happy? "It doesn't matter," she said. "Don't be Continental." And these were the words that made me lose my mind over her. A world in which it doesn't matter whether you feel good or bad as long as you can keep laughing: I had never seen it before. This was not the same laughter I knew at school; it was the real thing—a laugh that ignored any thing and any emotion designed to prevent it.

The idea that laughter might be caused by madness and all kinds of hysteria is not alien to the Freudian world in which I grew up. The big difference sat in front of me in red ankle socks; the difference between our Continental, Freudian way of categorizing the times, opportunities, states of mental health and financial situation eminently suitable for laughter, and laughing at any time, was called Elizabeth and I loved her immediately and without the slightest hesitation. If anyone could pull me out of my mourner's rut, it would be this girl, that was clear. I seemed to have found someone I could talk to, someone who didn't take serious matters too seriously, someone who shrugged her shoulders at miserable memories because they were too remote to be understood. The difference between England and Europe is not a channel but a thousand years of permanent war in which everything, every stone you step on, has been turned upside down by innumerable armies of liberators; hence my attraction to her. She would also be the first English-speaking girl I took to bed, and immediately after the party was over I suggested it. She reminded me of Dinah waiting for me at home; but before Dinah left I would have a chance to convince myself that this time I had not made a mistake. This time, I thought, the real Elizabethan era would dawn for me and only end when I died. It was that strong. She challenged all my ideas about the heaviness of this life (she called me "heavy" to tease me). When I told her that I pitied poor Dinah for having to leave, she said, "Sorry for her and not for yourself—are you sure?"

It was the other way of looking at it, a more introspective, more psychoanalytical way than my mind was used to. Freud left Vienna in '38 and converted more Anglo-Saxons to his ideas in the one year of his remaining life in London than he

94

had found followers in Vienna in his previous sixty-odd years as a doctor of the mind. The Viennese in me didn't believe that Freud had succeeded in Glasgow. How could I feel sorry for myself if I said I felt sorry for Dinah? She suggested that this was due to hypocrisy on my part; she in fact, but slowly, convinced me that I was lying and didn't really feel sorry for Dinah. What I had wanted to say could I have said it in Viennese was: *"Sie tut mir leid"*—"She causes me grief." And Elizabeth was perfectly right: I felt sorry for my own grief.

My first encounter with the Anglo-Saxon world was my meeting with our own Professor Freud, for whom I, as a true Viennese, had very little respect. I didn't really believe in his psychoanalysis; I thought it was just a system for putting the mind back in working order so the person could pursue his business again. (And is this not so?) To my mind every human being had only one business in the world, and that was to stay away from the dreadful treadmill called "making money." As long as one does not make money one is a free man, and it doesn't matter in which country one lives, under which political system, and it doesn't matter whether one is rich or poor, sick or healthy, black or white. You want to be either in or out. If you want to remain out, don't listen to Freud, don't let yourself get cured; there is nothing to cure but Freud's madness.

I loved Elizabeth instantly because she was affected by the analytical mind process that queries everything from the weather to the color of the rainbow. I called it the Jewish mind, which had obviously infected everyone from New York to Glasgow, from London to Melbourne, and so around the world. I was in a period when I still stupidly identified Jews with Jewish and Gentiles with Gentile mind. Elizabeth, who

95

didn't like Jews, she said, looked immediately as if she was going to be the one to convert me to them. She was from a large Catholic working-class family, with many sisters and brothers and a father who had worked in the Clydeside shipyards and was now either retired or unemployed, she was not sure which. Everything she told me was news from a new world. After Dinah went back to Amsterdam, we had all the time to ourselves, and now for the first time I didn't pursue other women, nor did I go out and drink alone with friends. I converted to a happy husband who was constantly in reach; all she had to do was call for me.

To laugh at everything and to be cruel to oneself by revealing one's own self-pity was only part of the lesson; her better instruction was to teach me to look after myself. She hated, and couldn't afford, to have me around penniless. She put it in my mind that I was growing up and it was about time I did something—I knew she meant making money. She said, "Why aren't you a Jew?"

Why was I not a Jew? Because I was convinced that being Jewish was a waste of time. What does it matter if you gather the entire wealth of this world together in this life when there is no next world to spend it in. I would much rather have been a Catholic, a real one, not as she believed in it. ("Me? Catholic? You mean am I going to church? Not if I can help it.") I wanted to be a real Catholic, one who has a savior on the cross and a heaven to go to. Elizabeth talked me out of this madness and wanted me to be a Jew, but to be a Jew is nothing one can learn (I thought); it has to come by itself or it never happens. I told her what I had told my brother-in-law, Alex. "I don't have to be a Jew. I'm one already."

She said, "You are crazy."

Crazy or not so crazy, if all things are equal it's better to be in bed with Elizabeth's laugh than with Dinah's disapproving looks. I even began to like it at the Academy, now that I had found my new mission, though I remained skeptical of the whole idea of the way we studied drama. Why pay for the bad bons mots of a Bernard Shaw and the baroque hogwash of a Giraudoux? What a theater! My pet distaste was for everything written by Christopher Fry, who became famous overnight. Authors such as Fry survived in the cold war literary establishment. Is the lady for burning? How should poor Viennese and naïve Americans know? They paid a lot to see a murder in a cathedral, but more, talked about this trash at school. The idea reminded me of Agatha Christie in beachcomber shorts, let loose on culture-hungry suburbia. All theater was bad except *Porgy and Bess,* which was a good operetta with a lousy story. I queued up for *Don Giovanni* and *The Magic Flute* as a new convert to opera if not to Judaism, and even standing for six hours, four of them in the queue in snow and rain, was better than going to anything else in town. I began to listen to Mozart's operas, Gluck's *Orfeo* and Schubert's *Requiem.* The theater was Nestroy. Nestroy was the one and only exception. Nestroy is the Austrian genius, the grand master of all theater hocus-pocus. He dances, he doesn't walk. He has a melody, a sound of his own. He is melancholic and loves the world, a sick, skeptical, torn-in-half, sentimental, optimistic, frightened-to-death wit; an amusing, elegant, childish old wise man. Nestroy and Mozart are the only Austrians I admired without reservations, and because of them I tried to inhale some of the divine magic that hangs over a country where a Nestroy and a Mozart could exist and Elizabeth had come to study singing. On certain days I felt it in the air. In spite of the cruelty and madness of the citizens, which is all

I had noticed so far, or because of it, I smelled a psychedelic type of ozone that transforms reality into magic.

I began to love it in town, but felt I should hate everyone and everybody. In the end I couldn't. They are Viennese, they are sick, there is no cure for it, and I am one of them. Either go away and never turn back, or like it here. No one was waiting for me anywhere. Going to the United States, as accidentally suggested by Mike Mabry, gave me the creeps. I didn't want to go to a country that had a government infantile enough to think it could defeat the communists and change the world. A country where slums and elegant skyscrapers grew side by side trying to defend the West in Korea? Not only their political ideas struck me as childish; their plays seemed to have been written for morons, though *Death of a Salesman* could be a turning point for America, I hoped. Confronted with the nakedness of his dream, the American citizen becomes human, a frightened European again. Are they ever going to learn that there are people in the world who prefer an un-American way of life? Even in 1952 the Nixons were losing the war in Asia, and no money, no atomic power and no CIA could prevent it. Who needed America then? My creditors did. I turned pro-West when I realized how expensive life was.

One Saturday afternoon, the revelation came as I sat on a bench in the Stadt Park, staring at a schilling piece in my hand. Once gone, this schilling was gone forever, and there was no chance of another one in the forseeable future. At this moment I decided it was time to change all that too. I didn't want to think about money ever again; I was sick of it. I had to leave here. I had to get out. A few days' work here and there was not good enough. With nothing to lose but a single schilling, I could afford to leave. Being a director, I decided, was too much work with too many stupid people; the best thing was to find a free man's occupation. I went to see David Perlman. Perlman taught me the rest: "Sorry, I don't have any money."

"What about all the money you play the stock market with?"

"That's money for making money. I don't have a penny. I'm as poor as you."

He found two schillings in his pockets and gave me one and said, "I am sharing my last schilling with you. Do you understand what this means?"

Walking back the three miles to save the schilling for bread, it clicked. Either I look after myself or I'll depend on him. Either I do what I want or I'll have to take what I get. If I'd like to be a writer, all I have to do is write and publish. I bought three slices of bread in a pub, went back home and never stopped writing, but somehow I got lost in the middle of a yarn, had no idea why I had started a story nor how I would end it.

PART THREE

There are apprentices in search of a master who leave home for a drink around the corner and disappear forever. They dip into a glass and are gone, write a book and vanish into their own fiction. A dimension of their minds becomes flesh. This is what happened to me in the summer of '53. My destination was the heart of all Egyptian fleshpots, a fabulous golden city in the north, fabulous because it had known nothing but peace and prosperity for centuries, miraculous because it seemed beyond all horizons. I had wanted to go to Stockholm ever since, as a child, I'd read about Nils Holgersson's miraculous journey on gooseback, by Selma Lagerlöf, the Swedish mystic. The little boy Nils Holgersson dismounted, I remembered, with northern solemnity on top of Mount Zion; this was long before I had seen the real Jerusalem of heat, unemployment and ordinary people. I wanted to take the same goose north because, as I saw it, Nils Holgersson came from the golden Jerusalem and could have stayed home. I would be up there sooner or later to tell him all about it, a long series of stories, some not so funny.

There are apprentices who never leave their studies yet fill the world's libraries with descriptions of journeys through infernos and paradisos, managing to take gullible readers on long trails to the far ends of the world. From their writing desks they guide them through cities of a pilgrim's progress and over the highlands of beautiful-sounding poetry. If I had had my own study in Vienna I might have mounted a telescope at my window and looked at the journey to Stockholm ahead, which would have saved me time and trouble hitchhiking there.

Erich Müller, the second person who sent me up north, was a different type of mystic. He was a painter who lived in a garret provided by a Viennese progressive priest. He was maybe a number of phases ahead. Stockholm, we agreed, is a a phase of mental development, just as Vienna is one, and Jerusalem another. Erich was ahead of me, trying to pull me after him into the loony bin of Steinhof. While I was still afraid I might not have enough luck or small change ever to make it to Sweden—which is no real fear but just anxiety before seeing something new—he watched his fingernails. On each one he saw a secret agent of the OGPU looking at him, trying to arrest him and drag him off to Vorkuta, Siberia, for what he had done during the war. "What did you do during the war?" His story was as pathetic as it was convincing—the mere sight of him made it that. Born in Yugoslavia of German-Yugoslav parents, a *Volksdeutscher*, he had to join the Waffen SS—the military, not the political arm of the SS—shortly before the end of the war. The Waffen SS caused a lot of havoc, particularly in eastern Europe. The very name SS gives everyone the shivers. But Erich had only been in it for the last two months of the war, a trainee murderer so to speak, a young art student who had never wanted to shoot anyone, who was himself scared of firearms, who loved people and hated Nazis. Yet there he was, with this record of having been in the SS—and whatever he said to anyone, he never forgot to mention this short-lived training, and people either turned away from him, spat in front of him, or left him sitting alone to watch his fingernails and drink himself to death.

I believed Erich. I sympathized with him. We were friends. Both survivors of a catastrophe, with the nice twist of the former SS man begging the Jew on his knees (he went on his knees many times; probably learned it from his priest protector) to believe that he was a good man.

"You sit there on this chair and judge me. You must believe me. If you don't, how will you believe anyone in this town who doesn't fall on his knees?"

A subtle argument. "I am no judge, Erich. You know what you didn't do, but do you know what you try to do? I believe you, but it makes no difference. You are afraid of the Russians, not the Jews."

Believe me, don't believe me; I was ready to believe him. The Russians chased Nazis, but among the Jews, apart from Simon Wiesenthal and a few helpers, no one did. And Erich was no Nazi. He said that Stockholm, where he had just come back from, was the finest town in the world, had the finest lakes, the finest food, the largest beds and the most interesting woman in it. "Her name is Robin," he said. "She is from New York, lives in Stockholm permanently, is waiting for you." It sounded like the fleshpot of all fleshpots, where the flesh would hang out of my mouth as a dry tongue in search of a single drop of truth. I raked up three months' scholarship in advance, a membership in the International Youth Hostel Federation in case Robin was not at home. I fixed a time to meet Elizabeth in Lugano (she first had to sing in the Bad Aussee opera festival) and mounted my goose.

The first night I made it to Innsbruck in the Tyrol, a romantic-looking hinterland of beautiful mountains and long-bearded peasants known for their stubbornness and independent ideas. Tyroleans had done something none of the other Austrian tribes had done. They had fought a rebellion against the Hapsburg overlords. Their people's hero, a forerunner of all Fidel Castros, is the bearded Andreas Hofer, of whom we learned in a song in school that he was executed by a firing squad. Tyrol stayed with the crown in Vienna, but the Tyroleans gained a taste of freedom the rest of the empire never had. Tyroleans love drinking, eating, dancing and singing. They can yodel, I found out, which is surprising, as they have two-way radios between cattle stations in the mountains there. Tyroleans are not Viennese. They are rough, tough, cordial and not false, perverted, cruel and suspicious as people are in Vienna. They speak about Tyrol's freedom and love no one who was not born in the Tyrol; they are never sick and tired of seeing only themselves around. One night in Innsbruck was enough. I didn't see what I could possibly do there if I stayed but eat, drink, yodel and talk Tyrolean politics. There must be Tyrolean writers who have something to say on the deeper layers of the Tyrolean soul. I didn't meet them. Local writers always find something unique in their town and I left as soon as possible, before I might find out that Innsbruck too is the cradle of the world.

About lunchtime the next day I crossed into Liechtenstein, tried in vain to persuade the police at the border to let me have their real stamp on my passport, which they kept, I suggested, for privileged travelers only. My stamp didn't mention Liechtenstein by name; it just said: *Pass.* I was disappointed to learn that they have an economic union with Switzerland, meaning they insured their patriotic Liechtenstein gesture—the prince, the moat and a few soldiers—in Zurich and Geneva. Liechtensteinians will never taste the freedom of the Tyroleans, who can fight and lose every time yet remain a people one can respect, while Liechtensteinians are a Swiss joke for foreigners. There was nothing I could do here. No Artclub, no women, no discussion. Pass.

Chur—the name made me want to go there. The German word *Kur* ("healing") is not the same thing. This Chur heals with prettiness. There was nothing but prettiness in this town. Everything and everybody was pretty: the shops, the streetcars, the people. Even the cats in the bushes and the parks breathed kind goodwill to anyone who was ready for it. I was tempted by Chur. Nice idea to find a quiet room in a quiet street among quiet neighbors, sit down and write a masterpiece, surprising all the world with so much exciting horrible mind filtering through pretty streets and alleys. That same night I stayed at the youth hostel, full of straight and less straight boy scouts; next day I answered a window ad for an assistant to a graphic artist. I started immediately after lunch. By 4 P.M. Mr. Spaehi, though he liked my company and my stories, offered me ten francs so I wouldn't remember anything nasty of him. "The drawing of the letter A is something very difficult. It takes a year to learn to draw just one single letter." For the B, I might have needed two years, for the C another seven, et cetera, et cetera, and the entire alphabet could probably not be learned before the grave. " 'Here rests J.L., a master of letter writing.' Sorry, Mr. Spaehi. I thought I could make it."

"Thank you for coming and please take this ten francs. Believe me, it's difficult. But you have talent."

"Thank you, Mr. Spaehi."

"Thank you for trying to help me."

Switzerland was a new language. In Austria a Mr. Spaehi would have pierced me with a dirty look until I had left voluntarily without even daring to consider opening my mouth either in protest or to say good-bye. Switzerland was a heaven of pretty streets and nice people; nothing more and nothing less. This is how it should be in the rest of the world. Pretty towns, nice people is the idea. I needed excitement. Something wild, mad going on. In Chur you sleep, eat and die. Nothing happens. (As if that wouldn't be enough to fill a lifetime!)

One could live two or three days on ten Swiss francs, the way I lived, but not more than an hour in Saint Moritz. No student bellhops, waiters, cleaners, graphic artists, private detectives required. The Italians did everything cheaper and better. I wanted to spend one single night in Saint Moritz to look at the fabulous rich, just to see what they looked like, and couldn't. I found the cheapest inn outside the town, took a bed in the "*Mauseturm*," and walked back to the playground at night—when everything was closed for me: drinks so expensive as to keep traveling apprentices away from the rich. My only chance was a tall and very pale German businessman who suggested putting me up for the night in the Grand Hotel. As I wasn't interested in getting that close to wealth, I refused. I wanted to listen at the bar; I wanted to know if what Fritz Brösel had claimed was true: "They are ordinary people just like you and me."

Among the vagrant Italians and other assorted travelers I felt at ease, and as the rich hate to give a hitchhiker a lift, afraid their cars might get dirty, there was no way out of this Shangri-La but by bus through the valley of Maloya. On the bus I met again the Italian workers I knew from my hotel. Snow-topped mountains, clear brooks, flowering meadows, majestic forests on the roadside didn't cheer them up. They looked grim and depressed like a busload of miners traveling home through a Welsh suburb. Scenery was obviously not enough to make them look happy. But if scenery is not enough, what is? The truth, not easily apprehended, hung upside down like a chicken from the luggage rack; to stand on my head (as I did most of the time) helped me to grasp some of it: It doesn't matter whether a trip takes three months, three years or the rest of my life. There is nothing to run away from and much to be gained by looking around. J.L. the survivor ended in a ditch between Saint Moritz and Lugano. The man next to me, who worked on a new hotel up in the mountains above Saint Moritz and was on his way to see his mother in the hospital, called it the valley of Paradise. At the mention of the word *Paradiso* he immediately smiled and looked bitter. He told me the wages were high and the work not too heavy, but the future grim all the same. He would never be able to afford as much as a garret for a single night in the new hotel he was at work on. Paradiso is also an Inferno if you have to water trees instead of sleeping underneath them, as the rich seem to do all the time. "I'm not a communist, mister; I'm just depressed."

I was in time to collect Elizabeth at the railway station. Her silliness seemed heavier than the two suitcases I carried for her up to the pension above town. Our love was probably over, but for the first time we could lie in bed together and fantasize that the mountains and Lake Lugano were our private property. I had not fallen out of love with her but fallen in love with the rest of the world. Concretely speaking, this meant I had stopped thinking that to be alive and to enjoy oneself was a major crime. Three hot days in Lugano and I gradually felt the healing hand wiping out all the nightmares of past nights in small strange towns. Now I could say I had been a sick man. My mind had been destroyed because of the war. In July '53 I felt the convalescence like a warm southern breeze. All I had to do was meander along the shore of Lake Lugano, look at nothing, just wander around, sit down and look, stare into the circles within circles a little pebble can create, and all was well.

In three days we went through all our money. Stockholm seemed neither feasible nor necessary. Yet we couldn't stay in Lugano. The landlady, used to richer and lazier travelers, was surprised we left the best swimming and fishing in Ticino so soon, without even a taxi to the railway station. God knows what Elizabeth carried around with her in those two suitcases. They weighed at least forty pounds each. To carry them out of town to the first possible auto stop sobered me. Elizabeth walked behind, complaining about the heat, her feet, her thirst, her stomach, her head and her own stupidity in ever meeting me in the first place. I didn't reply, as we still had eight hundred kilometers to Paris ahead.

In the first car, with two elegant homosexual Frenchmen from Dijon, we left a mark of unrefinement: we spilled a full bottle of red wine over their white hand-knitted seat covers and had to leave immediately. In the second car, with a young Swiss couple crossing the French Alps, we tried to make up for our mistake by playing sophisticated world travelers full of funny stories and anecdotes. The third lift was in a long-distance truck from Marseilles to Paris. The driver only needed to feel female knees next to his to prove the point he repeated for four hundred kilometers: "One single good-looking broad next to the driver is a better infusion than low-grade diesel fuel in the engine." I wished he had kept her with him. We arrived in Paris starved, exhausted, dirty. Elizabeth went to have a bath in the house of a girl friend from Vienna, an Armenian soprano named Yolande; managed to get a ticket out of the British consul on the empty promise that she would pay it back in Glasgow; and left.

No girl friend made me even happier than no money. I preferred living on the occasional hunk of bread a truck driver would share with me. Now on the road again, I liked this total freedom I had nearly forgotten, of owing the world nothing. That's the way it should be. Free of suitcases, the mind travels light. Not until Amsterdam would I be able to borrow a cent. In Amsterdam, Ditta, my younger sister, would help me. She had been reconvalescing from a thigh she broke when her truck blew up on a mine in the first battle over Jerusalem in 1948. Her thigh had healed and she stayed on in Amsterdam, working at the Israeli embassy, before she went back a few years later. She would somehow manage to get me on the road to the far north. I couldn't make Paris–Amsterdam in one day. Glad to make it to The Hague, I planned to stay overnight with Batist, the only children's nurse I had kept in contact with since the days of Ockenburgh, the refugee camp, back in 1939. Batist had been everyone's favorite. She had been a friend, not merely a nurse. She had loved the children—she had none of her own—and her marriage was a mess after the war. I was sure she would be happy to put me up for the night. It was nearly dark when I arrived at her door. A tiny old woman opened and told me to go away because Henny Batist was dying. "She is in a coma and it's only a matter of hours." I insisted I would like to see her, and the old woman, a neighbor, let me come upstairs to see for myself. The room was nearly dark, the curtains drawn. I didn't want to believe that Batist, who was in her mid-thirties, was dying.

I stood in the room, looked at her. She didn't see me. I said my name twice. She seemed to open her eyes. She called my name. I couldn't understand anything else. She talked in a language of her own, something no one needs to understand. The little old woman, who had spent the past few days with her, told me to run for a doctor (there was no telephone in the house). I ran downstairs and all the way to the doctor's, but he wasn't at home. I left a message and ran back to say the doctor should be coming soon. "It's too late now. She is dead. It was hopeless anyway. A brain tumor."

"Where are you staying?" As I didn't know, she suggested that I stay at her place. Her husband was in an old age home. There was an empty bed. There were two empty beds, in fact. Her son was married and lived in Australia. I wanted to leave but the old woman insisted I stay. "You can't go anywhere tonight; better stay here." I had a bath, slept next day until noon, and she made me breakfast. "Let me tell you something. When you came to the door last night and it was nearly dark, I knew I had to put you up for the night, and I didn't even know who you were, but it says in the Holy Scriptures: If a stranger comes to your door after dark, don't

112

let him go away. He may be your Lord Jesus Christ. I am sure Batist was happy to see you before she died. God bless her soul. And God bless you on your road!"

The only town I felt at home in was Amsterdam. I love its winter, its autumn and spring, but above all I love it there during the summer. Summer in Amsterdam is an extended lit-up celebration of bridges and canals. They hadn't stopped drinking at Eylders and Reinders just because I had left for Vienna. The same people sat on the same chairs, as if I had just gone to the urinal. I was back. Everyone said, "Where have you been?" The same old girls but also a few new faces. It looked as if it would be good for me to stay here for a few weeks. I had friends; I knew people who knew people who knew of a room for very little money or even nothing if I would stay in two or three nights a week and baby-sit. A room for free in the Beethovenstraat. Not the most interesting part of town, but private, under the attic, and I had my own key. That's all I needed to collect a dozen or so girls within the first few days. Bed was still the most interesting of all spiritual adventures as far as I could judge the situation of man versus the universe. One could waste much time discussing the world or on the study of wise and holy books; one could enlighten oneself by watching a Fellini or a Visconti movie; one could go to a new Sharoff production of *The Seagull*—or one could stay in bed. It made no difference. Study doesn't improve the brain and enlightenment is ultimately boring. I was not really interested in anyone's fantasy but my own. Drinking can be done in between fantasies, but the main thing was definitely getting close enough to a female, preferably an attractive one, not only to sort out her past and predict her future, but to feel her presence. To feel meant to

113

me: feel the reality. Don't talk about it, don't philosophize about it, don't listen to other people's descriptions of it. Listen to yourself. One good-looking audience in bed is worth two thousand in an auditorium. Fucking was not the purpose but the crowning of every excursion into this fantastic no-man's-land of cunt, ass, lips, tits, kisses, talk, tears, laughter. Maybe one has to be ordinary and normal, as I always thought myself to be; maybe one has to be one of the people in the true sense of the word and not an artist or genius or superior person—just Everyman looking for Everywoman—and the mystical union can take place. Being a "true artist" might have something to do with curbing his genital interests. Syphilis worked for Nietzsche and probably Ibsen, but not for everyone.

It depended on whom I would meet in Amsterdam. The second or third day I found Elsa, the daughter of a policeman from the vice squad—nineteen, pink-cheeked, untouched, but she ruined it for me by taking her clothes off within seconds and hanging them neatly over a chair, lying down on the bed and saying, "If that's what you want, go ahead and do it then!" After ten minutes she was up and cheerful, took her bicycle and was off. I visited Dinah again, but Dinah smiled at my suggestion as if I had lost my mind. Miep was in town, all right for bed, but to listen to her drove me mad. Her breakfasts were good and I stayed with her for two days. Bep, the wife of a friend, was at home, but she had three children and very little time. I could have an hour a day (after three and preferably before six, when Piet came back from the office). He might have joined us in bed; she liked the idea, I didn't. One man in bed was enough. Connie too had married while I was away. Her husband insisted that I stay with his wife, as he had "other things to do."

I finally found what I wanted sitting on the stairs at a

114

cabaret show in the old town. That evening she had to go back
to her mother, as otherwise the old lady might be waiting up
for her all night. Next day at five she came in a very thin
silken dress, to get to it quicker. I suggested making coffee,
but found there was no sugar in the house, went down and
across the road to get the sugar, and came back with Sonya.
Sonya undressed Grete within thirty seconds, stretched her
out on the couch and buried her tongue right up her before I
could say, "What's going on?" With some difficulty I got
Sonya to dress and allow Grete to put on her pants just so we
could go one floor higher up, since the couple I was staying
with was about to come home. "Do they sleep with you?"
Sonya asked. Hardly in my room, Grete was stripped again,
and Sonya again all over her. A new kind of love. I timed
it. Fifty-five minutes exactly. It took me another fifteen
minutes to get Sonya out of the house. Erna was an amateur
compared to Grete, and if Grete was better than Erna, there
might be someone still better waiting for me in Hamburg,
and then one even better in Copenhagen, while the supreme
woman was probably this Robin in Stockholm, of whom Erich
had said, "She is real class." Which in Viennese means "first
class."

I didn't care for Hamburg now, largely rebuilt since I had
seen it last in May 1945. I hated their Reeperbahn, a deaden-
ing affair of drunks and tarts, clip joints and gangsters. I was
sad and depressed in Germany. The man in the cot next to
me in the youth hostel sighed and jerked off all night. It was
hot in the dormitory.

Copenhagen was new land. Not knowing a soul in this town
made it much more exciting. Copenhagen was peaceful, as if
it lived before 1914, drunk as if it were a matter of principle,

frivolous and an easy place to make friends. All you had to do was stand still on a corner and someone wanted to show you the road; all you had to do was smile and everyone smiled back. No language needed, and no introduction. The first evening I knew everyone in the local artist taverns and the second I was an old friend. (That was before pot threw people into quiet corners to meditate on their own brains.) The third night I looked through a window and saw a laughing crowd (Danes always laugh) drunk around a huge table, and within minutes I sat at the same table, as if I had found lifelong pals. Telling Jewish jokes was a way of making friends. For some reason Danes love Jews; I think because Jews seem exotic to them. There was a single dark-haired girl at the table who must have been waiting for me at least ten years. "All my life," she said on our way through the botanical gardens. *Al bukra*, behind a bush, I found Copenhagen, the best place for me in the world. Marian wanted to introduce me to the theater director Sam Besekov and was ready to marry me as soon as I said O.K. Through her I met Hjort, who remained a friend for many years. Marian had soft silken skin, fucked even better than Erna and Grete, but she had two drawbacks. She lived at home with her mother and was a little too serious. Her friend Sam I liked instantly and he offered to make me his assistant at the theater if he could manage to get me a labor permit. I would hear more about it when I came back from Stockholm (he had been there during the war and no sane Dane expects anyone to stay in Stockholm). Marian also took me to Inger, who taught young ladies gymnastics and rhythmic dancing, giving a little massage on the side. Inger lived alone in a pleasant house on the outskirts and I was welcome at her place any time of night or day. Marian suggested that I stay with Inger, and joined me in bed when Inger went off to do things in town. The life of the sexual acrobat costs nothing and gives the opportunity to celebrate the end of the war and better days to come. After ten days I decided it was better not to be known around town as Marian's new husband.

Sweden is barely two hours but two thousand miles removed from Copenhagen and light-years from the rest of Europe. It impressed me as a sad silence. People didn't speak, even children didn't laugh and shout in the street; they were not like children anywhere else in the world. Sweden was self-containment, self-control and self-pity. But mainly self-control. No one moved a face muscle (if he could avoid it), in order to impress his fellowman with his seriousness. The very week I arrived there had been a gruesome murder of a motorist by a hitchhiker dressed up as a girl. No one wished to pick up a student, and certainly not a foreign one. Late in the afternoon, before dark, a fat man picked me up for no apparent reason. He was a traveling salesman of plastic relief maps and didn't wish to talk to me. He didn't want to know who I was, where I came from or where I was going. Suddenly he mentioned he had to turn left, off the main road, and I stood in the nearly dark landscape, five miles' walk from the nearest town. (The silent fat man later turned into a hero in a short story. He became Balthasar, the cannibal in "Hurrah for Freedom.")

I was in Lund, a university town of which I had heard. I didn't know a soul. I had no addresses, and people from Lund didn't invite strangers to drink with them and sleep with their girls. Stockholm was still six hundred kilometers or so north.

The Chevrolet was steered by a young, unhappy-looking executive who had to marry a woman the same week and wanted me to make up his mind for him. "Shall I marry her or shall I emigrate?" I had to decide on his future before Norrköping. "On the one hand," I said (looking at his black mustache and summing him up as a playboy), "you will be sorry within a year; on the other hand, if you need a mistress on the side you can always come to see me in Vienna; I could fix you up." It was a wild and unexpected solution to his otherwise dreary prospect of spending married life in Norrköping. "It wasn't really what I dreamed of when I was still a student. I have a PhD in physics and chemistry, yet I'm a total idiot. I don't even know what to do tomorrow." Only much later, in the United States, did I meet people like this man, who were ready to tell a stranger the color of their bowel movement of that very same morning. Does it have something to do with a high standard of living when people are afraid they may always be doing the wrong thing? Or was it I, who collected any story, who just made them talk. As long as the story didn't omit any detail, I was a good listener; the smallest detail is the essence of the story and it makes a huge difference whether Sven's mother is sixty-five and can pay for her own meals or whether she is seventy-five and poor. Sven's mother was old and rich and she held the winning hand. He knew he had to marry. Sven thanked me for all the things I had pointed out, said it was better and cheaper to talk to a stranger on the road than to go to a psychiatrist, which gave you a reputation of mental imbalance right away in a small town like Norrköping. As to the girls I offered him in Vienna, he was certainly going to see me there soon.

The Royal Café near the Dramatten, where I found Robin the same night, was by all Artclub and Eylders standards the quietest café in the world. No alcohol. Swedes are not allowed to drink too much or they might turn into savage Slavic Vikings after the fifth aquavit, their government thinks. Robin was better than I expected. Erich was right. First of all, she was from New York and I understood her right away. Her company was a sad-eyed Welshman, Sam Goldsmith, who left Cardiff because people had been teasing him as long as he could remember. "Everyone in Cardiff says, 'Come on, Sam, why don't you admit it, of course you are a Jew. With that nose.' I have a big nose, my name is Sam Goldsmith, but I am not a Jew."

"Come on, Sam, why don't you admit it. . . ." I don't know if this joke would have made me leave Cardiff. I wouldn't have left Vienna in '38 had the Viennese not taken the Jewish question so seriously and burned us whether we admitted being Jewish or not.

When she was not making her leather bags, and not busy with her son, or when she did not have to see Sam ("I feel sorry for him, he is so sad"), I saw Robin. Erna was good, Grete better, Marian better than that, and Robin the best. She didn't think of marrying anyone. She worked hard to remain independent. Stockholm was a town and not a honey cake Jerusalem, and I didn't want to get trapped in regular work. No Robin, no Marian, no Dinah, no Ida—no Jewish woman, in fact—will ever respect a man who doesn't look after her, or is not capable of doing so even if he doesn't want to. All women are women. All women want you to settle down. All women want one man only and don't allow another woman around, as if they were speaking for Jehovah Himself, who couldn't stand other gods around. The relation between God and woman wasn't all that clear to me

119

back in '53, but something must have dawned on me. Love supreme is interlocked with body and soul, in woman and mind. Robin made it easy; she treated me as a friend and made no claims on my time. She was the best woman I had met so far in my life.

Did I leave her place under my own steam or did she suggest I'd better move on? I waited in the queue of a student restaurant on the Kungsgatan and offered a free lunch to the first good-looking girl who would put me up for the night. The first one I asked, Alexandra, was ready for the deal. She was red-haired, blue-eyed, and couldn't possibly suggest settling down. Our situation was similar. I had no roof over my head and she had nothing to eat. She ate so little for lunch that I feared she might have fallen in love with me right away. After lunch I walked her to her place. To judge by the smiles and jokes she had for every male student between eighteen and forty we passed, she knew all of Stockholm. She lived in a small single room without bathroom or kitchen on the ground floor of a large building in a quiet street. She shared her bed with her cousin Sophia, a student nurse. (That Sophia could not be a tyrannical dyke like Sonya I could judge from her picture on the mantelpiece.) "You can sleep on a mattress; we have another mattress. How do you like the idea?"

By seven or so Sophia arrived. She was dark and had dark eyes. The two didn't look like cousins, but as they behaved like cousins, the situation looked better than I could have anticipated. Alexandra was not always at home, Sophia might be home without her cousin; in this case it would be wise to share my favors equally. It was the first week of September. The days were getting cool, the evenings cold, and I was broke.

It lasted two days. Sophia left at six in the morning for her work, and as they had literally nothing to eat, Sophia (I saw it with my own two eyes) tore a few sheets of white paper into strips and ate them. "That's my breakfast." I thought it was a circus trick. "I have eaten paper for many years. It's good and nourishing." I bought them breakfast. After Sophia left I joined Alexandra in bed. She didn't stop singing *"Deutschland, Deutschland über Alles."* Her story started in Lithuania, where both cousins were born and from where they went to Berlin during the war. The defeat of Berlin forced the family to come to Sweden, where life was sadness and poverty compared to the good old days under Hitler, when Lithuanians in Berlin could get good Jewish shops and apartments, she said.

My problem with Alexandra was not to turn a healthy but stupid girl into an antifascist; my problem was how to get a hand and subsequently the rest of myself into this young Lithuanian Nazi movement. It was impossible. She was convinced that I, as an intelligent person, must be an Austrian Nazi, as we can't all be Lithuanian Nazis, but she was afraid of her mother, who had sworn she would break her bones if she found out that Alexandra had no hymen left to hook a rich American oil executive with. I found the story very unlikely and suggested that her mother would never find out, and probably no millionaire in the world cared nowadays for hymens. Alexandra wasn't to be convinced. The world, she said, could not be that bad, even America, which on the whole was a moral dungheap because of its huge Jewish population. In good time I could have made a left wing, bohemian, cosmopolitan, philo-semitic tramp out of her, but it might have taken the same effort as settling down with Marian, Elizabeth, Robin, Dinah, Ida.

121

I left Stockholm the next day, after a sleepless night on the mattress listening to the breathing of the cousins. I had to leave because mother was coming to town the same day, probably to check Alexandra and Sophia with a flashlight. After Copenhagen I had second thoughts about whether Stockholm was the original of all Egyptian fleshpots. It seemed more an upside down glass bowl that trapped its inhabitants in a life of permanent social security and boredom. I wasn't ready for this. The mind thrives only where the past is a mess, the present a bet on unlikely probabilities, and the future uncertain. The democratic and social security road I was ready to recommend now more than ever to workers, employees and hunting and fishing barons, but not to people who sailed their goose in the sky.

PART FOUR

PART FOUR

Back in Copenhagen, Marian was still in love with me—in fact, now more than ever, as she'd never expected to hear from me again. Love silenced her. All she could do was look at me, nodding her head in admiration and disbelief; her palms moistened when she held my hand and her eyes filled with tears when I said I wouldn't wait for a labor permit from the Danish home office, as this might take another seven years. Copenhagen was the original Egyptian fleshpot and the ultima Thule of my journey. Beyond this country of Denmark there were no people kinder, friendlier, more humane and better fed. Yet the smell of grease and bulging fatty tissue, of gravy and meat in the air, ruined my stomach. I began to feel sick—I had to throw up. I left Marian in the middle of a performance of the Royal Ballet, whispered something about the cloakroom, picked up my bag there before the lights came on, and left. As a kind of final impression of Denmark to take home with me, a traveling salesman showed me pictures of his wife and a little Moroccan girl, their au pair, trained to serve the morning tea in bed and not just leave it at the bedside table. "In my country there is little else to do but fornicate. Our state does everything else for us."

My real problem was obviously in my mind. There wasn't much in the world I could change. I had to change something inside my brain first. This traveling and fucking had to stop. I was getting tired of it. Celebrations of victory had to come to an end, and the time was ripe to do something more useful. But what exactly? If the most useful thing is breathing, is there anything else one can do? Something for others maybe? But what, and for whom? I counted the possibilities on my fingers, and dismissed them one by one. Politics was out, as I couldn't think of any party or program worth wasting a single hour on. The theater was out, unless I began to write my own plays and maybe even act in them and direct them. But writing was out too. Writing needed time, more time than I could find between jobs. There was no job I could think of that would fit me besides night watchman, sailor or spy. These I was doing, actually: staying up all night, sailing from one port to the next with a cargo of varied sweets and a lot of heavy stones for balance, and spying out a Promised Land where I could settle more permanently (this happened anyway, and by the way). What's the point of making plans for years ahead, or even months ahead, if one or two pushes on some buttons can bring the whole universe crashing down on our heads? A family certainly seemed a full-time occupation and even an end in itself. Maybe I should marry Elizabeth and settle down wherever she liked—but that wouldn't work. No money, no settling down. And besides, she wanted fame, not family. How about my own fame? Didn't I want to be famous? It might have its practical advantages but not much more to recommend it. (It might get me theater tickets, for instance, when no one else could get them, or invitations to eat and drink with other famous people, but so what?) Maybe I should go to Canada as Fritz Brösel had always suggested, to be a woodcutter or a cowboy or something that took me away from urban problems. Or study philosophy in a monastery? Or religion? Or just do nothing—and fall asleep in a bathtub and drown? However, this last alternative didn't sound too exciting either.

From my notebook:
I liked nothing more than to be left in peace to think: I was a thinking-machine. Left alone, I thought up the most extraordinary things, while had I spent the same time talking to others, laughing with them, listening to their varieties of insanity, I would certainly have wasted my time. Life was an idea and a good idea providing you never let it slip out of your mind. My mind flew ahead and was on the summit before the body could sit down to sigh and puff. I was sitting on the top of a mountain and my thoughts were clear. The machine, in its best condition, can spell pure thought. Good mind. Perfect vision. How to get there? By wanting to be in peace, by climbing the mountain, sitting down and letting the rest happen by the machine.

Elizabeth was back and surprised to find me in town. She had given it considerable thought, she said, and decided there was no future for the two of us. (What future did she have in mind?) Her future was the opera, and to make it at the opera she needed four men: one man to back her immediately; one man to provide security in the long run; one man totally devoted; one who got her out of bed and to rehearsals

127

and sexually overexcited in the morning and listened to her pains and aches, moods and whims at all hours of the night and day. I was ready to listen to her, but not at all hours of night and day. When would I find time to peel my own onions? time to reflect? time for experimenting with pen and typewriter? She'd better marry a Jewish doctor (which she did a few years later). "I am what I am; take it or leave it." She wanted to leave it, yet couldn't quite see how (as good lovers are rare, she said). How could she leave me? How could I ever think of leaving her? If I wanted to leave her why didn't I, and if she wanted to leave me why did we see each other every free minute of the day to fight, bicker, quarrel, kiss, fuck and swear eternal love? Why did all this have to happen as in bad novels? Why was there no clear yes or no? Only torture, heartache, headache, pains and talk about dying together to get it over with. How could we have been so mad and perverted that we never stopped discussing the slightest emotional disposition? The main trouble between lovers is their need for jealousy. If absent, those symptoms will be produced automatically by a few words or gestures, a nod of the head, a look in the wrong direction, a silly joke, a lusty remark, a stupid misunderstanding. That's what "being in love" seemed to be all about—a pleasure in mutual torture. And if we had nothing else to fight about, we quarreled about money. We could fool ourselves into believing it was the world at large that was no good, yet to blame the world at large is not that easy; one has to be more specific than to say "them." Elizabeth was fairly good at giving "them" names. One was her teacher and conductor, Hans Swarovsky, who insisted that she not show up at rehearsal fifteen minutes later than everyone else. Another was the *Fürstin*, her landlady, a third her German teacher

(German is hard to learn for Scots), the fourth the high price for the room at the *palais*—and above everything and everyone she blamed me for having no money. She had to pay for our meals if she wanted to eat at a good restaurant. The more people Elizabeth knew to blame for our misery, the more I began to blame no one but myself (was I really innocent of not having inherited a mill, a factory or a house?). Her way of looking at the world as if it were a place one can buy I secretly admired. To wait and see and say "Perhaps" drove her nuts.

One late afternoon she locked herself in her room with a Norwegian music student called Stranger. I hammered at the door and threatened to kill her whether she opened up or not. She wasn't impressed. I heard sighing and heaving, bed-springs groaning. She shouted through the locked door that I should "go back to that Canadian cunt Rosalie." Instead I went down the corridor to the room of a giggling seventeen-year-old six-foot-tall Swedish girl named Barbara. Maybe I could fall in love with this Barbara. Barbara was willing to borrow my hand for her games (as she was tired of her own) but too afraid of Elizabeth to let me into her bed. All went well—very well—but suddenly Elizabeth screamed, "Open up and I'll kill you, you fucking son of a bitch. Open up immediately!" Barbara crawled away under her eiderdown. I said I would come out if she left the door first. She held a huge kitchen knife. I got it away from her and threw it out of the window. This impressed her. Afterward all was bliss and happiness. She swore on her mother's grave she had only pretended she was fucking Stranger to make me jealous. I swore I had never made it with Barbara. These promises were followed by hugs, kisses and a very hot bath, which was our daily routine after making love.

On a Wednesday we might have hated each other's guts; on Thursday morning we were as inseparable as two old pigeons. But how would we get through this winter?

Blow smoke to the ceiling, lie down in your bath and reflect —and maybe it will be clear. Whatever happens, it happens right in this brain. It all happens on top of this neck, on top of this face, inside this forehead and maybe a few inches higher up, but nowhere beyond these two fistfuls of gray gooey matter. The universe, all of it, is locked between two ears and covered with a film of skin underneath a mop of hair. And that's all. And no more. And nothing else. If I could learn to see through the smoke of a cigarette I could see everything ahead.

I went to see a friend who specialized in all things Chinese— incense, food, acupuncture, the *I Ching*—to see whether he could do something for me; if not, I was ready to treat him. Joseph was a medical student in his fourth or fifth year. He tore three pages from a copy of the *I Ching* which he kept for just such occasions and told me I had basically nothing to fear, neither now nor in the future. As the world is in safe hands now, the Chinese will soon introduce the Chinese *T'ai*—made of *K'un* the receptive earth and *Ch'ien* the creative heaven—and I could go home and take it easy. I should take the image of peace to my bath and think of it: heaven and earth unite in the following image of a universal peace:

> Thus the ruler
> divides and completes the course of heaven and earth;
> He furthers and regulates the gifts of heaven and
> earth,
> And so aids the people.

Heaven and earth are in contact and combine their influences, producing a time of universal flowering and prosperity. . . .

> Bearing with the uncultured in gentleness,
> Fording the river with resolution,
> Not neglecting what is distant,
> Not regarding one's companions:
> Thus one may manage to walk in the middle. . . .

> No plain not followed by a slope.
> No going not followed by a return.
> He who remains persevering in danger
> Is without blame.
> Do not complain about this truth;
> Enjoy the good fortune you still possess.

Everything on earth is subject to change. Prosperity is followed by decline. This is the eternal law on earth. Evil can indeed be held in check but not permanently abolished. It always returns. This conviction might induce melancholy, but it should not; it ought only to keep us from falling into illusion when good fortune comes to us. If we continue mindful of the danger, we remain persevering and make no mistakes. . . .

> He flutters down, not boasting of his wealth,
> Together with his neighbor,
> Guileless and sincere. . . .

> The sovereign I*
> Gives his daughter in marriage.
> This brings blessing
> And supreme good fortune. . . .

> The wall falls back into the moat.
> Use no army now.
> Make your commands known within your own town.
> Perseverance brings humiliation.

---

* Ch'êng T'ang, the first of the Shang rulers, whose reign is thought to have begun in 1766 B.C.

A few days later I went back to him, complaining that the wisdom of the *I Ching* didn't cheer me up.

"Doesn't cheer you up? If peace in the world doesn't, what ever will cheer you up? Your problem is the war; it's still on your mind—not Elizabeth but your fear of war. But if you have peace in the world, your main problem is solved. There are no more world wars to come; maybe a little killing here and there, but the big wars are over. From now on, love, justice and mercy will spread like the plague until the whole human race is infected by it. And there are no more feeble excuses of imperfect human conditions, all being relative. You'd better think again before you go on complaining."

Joseph suggested that I try to put down on paper my earliest impressions. I sat up a few nights to ponder about earliest impressions and came up with the following:

I was born on a big river. When I arrived the town was under six feet of snow and everything frozen up. The rivers, the water pipes, my mother's blood, my own blood, the moisture in my eyes. "The hardest winter ever," people said. The day I was born the Palace of Justice burned down to its foundations; there wasn't a drop in any of the twenty thousand firemen left that could have put the fire out. A cold winter indeed. The burning Palace of Justice was the only fire going in town; snow and ice prevented any transport of coal and wood. People fell forward like planks, frozen stiff, and were later unthawed together with thousands of elderly poor who had fallen asleep in their ice caves. I wonder whether there had been a winter like this before, but my impression is there could never be one like this again. Next time we would all die.

*My ascendant is Taurus and the zodiac was in Aquarius.
The year was '27, not that it matters. What matters: I was
born practically under the ice, slowly thawing toward the sun,
which stood in the west when I saw it first. It looked red and
warm on the white. At the age of thirty minutes I closed my
eyes, blinded by the color. (My being born with eyes
open is a family legend.) The smells in the room were
frozen. To recall any early unpleasant smells from the
people around me was impossible. Their frozen faces smiled;
there was no movement anywhere to disturb my new nervous
system. Life was a quiet affair muffled by ice and snow
outside.*

*Long before I crossed a ferry over a wide river I had to make
a decision and an effort a thousand times more difficult. To be
born is difficult, but even harder is to decide. I do not remember that "nature" instructed me when it was time to
leave but remember distinctly the colors red and white. To
"see" more of these colors, I knew I had to go ahead. The
colors shone from somewhere far away, yet were not un-
reachable. They were at the end of a dark shaft but distinctly
"there," and following my eyes, I pushed and propelled my
head and shoulders out of this furrow. It wasn't easy; the
passage was narrow, something held me back, something
didn't want me to leave, something pressed against my body,
held me in its grip, forced me to push forward because paus-
ing was agony. The pain drove me out. The colors in my eyes,
on my mind, caused the pain to start with. It wasn't just
hunger, as I had thought before. When I nearly reached the
end of the tunnel, I hesitated; a cold wind out there hurt the
skull, every root of my hair. To get a little used to the cold, I
kept my hair in the ice, and as the pain outside was less fierce*

than the pain in the rest of my body, I pushed my head farther, until my ears stuck out in the cold and my nose sniffed cold. My mouth was sealed, not to let any cold air in, and twisting my shoulder and stretching my arms and legs, I jumped forward—without a thought in my mind. What a relief! It was the best moment of my life—and there, behind walls of glass, were the red and the white. (Presumably our national flag.)

"A great and fine day for a great and fine fellow," someone said in the room. A great and fine fellow, yes, and one who couldn't keep his mouth shut. I screamed because I was immediately mad at everybody and everyone and maybe a bit mad at myself to have gone after the colors instead of staying where it was warm. "I'm freezing! I'm cold!" They went on touching my stomach, my soul. Someone squeezed my intestines. I bellowed a curse; it hurt like burning hell. Then there was a short click and a knot, which hurt as well, but nothing compared to the cold. I was happy for a moment and fell quiet. My soul was knotted up—I can still feel it. Someone rammed my intestines up my throat—I can still vomit when I think of it. Someone bashed my ass—I can still hear it in seconds of silence.

When Elizabeth read this she thought I had made it up and should be doing something more serious with myself—start looking for another place to begin with: the *Fürstin* was getting the idea I must be Jewish and wanted me out of the *palais*. A Jew in the house of an Austrian duchess is something strange. A Jew in the house is like a madman in the house. He turns people on with his weird ideas. I had suggested to her that she offer the use of her ballroom for performances by the Academy. This would give her three things: money, fame and a houseful of not uninfluential people. What more can a poor duchess want? My trouble was that I should not have talked to her to start with. I should have hated her (she was a well-known Nazi), but pitied her. Nothing was forgotten or forgiven; I just felt sorry for her. She had believed in a madness, the Hitlerian Teutonic-pagan madness, and it had cost her four sons. She had forced them to volunteer for the SS and they hadn't come back. I felt sorry for people who had lost their sons; hence I felt sorry for her. Maybe a little exaggerated, maybe not necessary, maybe too sentimental, maybe too religious? I don't know why I felt sorry for her; I just proved I was, by turning her mind to the idea of an auxiliary stage that would help her financially.

"Once you get this going, *Fürstin*, you never know where it will end." I brought a few friends along from the Academy. When she saw these young and handsome actors, with handsome names and daddys with money, she began to believe the ballroom could be used for a theater, yet she herself had never thought of it. She had given parties in this ballroom, rented it out for musical evenings, and had made a little money on the cloakroom. The moment she realized I was doing her a favor, she was convinced I must be Jewish, because according to current thinking Jews help others in order to enrich themselves in the process. That's good anti-Semitic thinking and I didn't care. I proved I had no interest in the whole thing by not pursuing the idea. Suddenly my room was promised to someone else; she had forgotten this when I moved in two months ago, she told Elizabeth. I had another address, of a baroness in the Mahlerstrasse (the quarters in the houses of impoverished aristocrats were usually larger and better furnished), and went to see the room.

It was ten times larger than I'd imagined, reached via a small winter garden and isolated from the rest of the house. It had a huge bed, a closet, a bathroom not too far away, hot water and a big writing desk and lamp. Looked just right for me. The Baroness was about eighty, veiled in black silk like Queen Victoria, and her daughter, roughly forty-five, was very tall, very fat, unattractive and shy. The daughter worked as a part-time translator for an American business-man, but as this wasn't enough to live on, she also taught English two hours a week and made dresses and pillow covers for special clients in the evenings. The two ladies observed me carefully. The mother sat in a wheelchair, the huge daughter stood next to her like an Austrian Statue of Liberty. The room had not been cleaned since the Baron died in 1908; it was dirty and it stank of mothballs. I knew this Baroness wouldn't like a "Jew" in the house either. A "Jew" would see right away what could be done to improve this mess (sell the furniture—by now antique—at a public auction). They looked at me with the eyes of their father and husband, Lud-wig von Lauchwitz, Austrian-Hungarian ambassador at the court of the Czar from 1902 to 1908, and finally decided in my favor. "But no company, please, after eleven P.M." In love with the huge desk in my room, I made sure everyone left before the ladies were up.

Having a desk to sit at under a lamp in a quiet house, I began to think about grammar. Not German or English grammar. But grammar. The particular twist of the mind that protects us against schizophrenia. Some kind of revelation, no doubt. How else could one know what I, you, he, she, it, we, you,

136

they is? I told my friend from America, David Bronson, what was on my mind, but he was more interested in the German language and in writing his PhD on the Austrian author Joseph Roth. If he ever tried to say something, it didn't reach me.

I talked to David's friend, a red-haired, bearded student of philosophy, who was happy to tell me everything he had just read. Did I want to know anything about Kierkegaard or Heidegger, Sartre or Camus? Ken was an existentialism specialist from Nebraska or North Carolina, but he didn't want to debate the revelation of grammar and I didn't see any point in discussing Sartre. Does the discussion of other people's ideas change the world? Or at least part of mine? Maybe, maybe not. There was no one else in Vienna to talk to, not in my orbit. Had I been famous, as famous as the philosopher Ernst Fischer, I thought, I would be allowed to talk to him, but not before. Victor Frankl, the Catholic-minded logo existentialist, was fashionable. After one lecture I thought he meant the Cardinal of Vienna or the Pope in Rome when he talked about God.

Action. The evening of Noel Coward's *Hands Across the Sea* didn't stir deep waters. The performance at the Academy came and went, watched by a number of friends and relatives of the students in our play. My name was on the program. Black on white. It said: *Regieassistenz . . . J.L.* My name in print. How to get one's name in print? The quickest way would be a stunt from a parachute above town. I lined up a job on a very bad illustrated weekly magazine, and attempted to translate terrible English love stories for Viennese housewives. Yet I couldn't really translate anything into anything. Either the humor escaped me or the pay wasn't adequate. After a few

137

days I gave it up to have more time for writing about translation:

My learning was of no avail. For ten years I entertained the people, here and everywhere else, with jokes and stories, just as my great-grandfather did, who used to make his living in front of a tent on the town's square on long summer evenings. (Some listen, some don't, all have a good time, he said.) Where did I go wrong with my jokes and stories? Haven't I explained every joke, repeated every story, twice and sometimes three times, for latecomers, hard-of-hearing old men and idiots who didn't understand what I was talking about? Unexplained humor is not considered funny around here. I tried it for a few years; no one knew whether to laugh or to cry. Only after I decided to throw in some explanations did I begin to get a little money. I couldn't afford silent smiles. For extra money I used to translate their jokes into our language and the other way round. I also translated novels, plays, short stories written in our peculiar idiom. There are not many people left in this world who can speak the two languages simultaneously, and that's why I always had plenty of work.

The translation of languages is a sacred and futile attempt to communicate between us and them, and more necessary than most people care to think. My translation work was probably much more important than anything else I did because there was not the slightest chance that anyone who could not speak our language as his mother tongue would ever be able to learn it. Many people tried; no one succeeded. It's not Turkish and not Tartar, not Russian and not Mongolian, not Jewish and not Armenian, not Slavic, not Arabic, not Magyar. In fact it has nothing in common with the 1,250-

138

odd known languages and dialects. Unless you are born in this republic that never existed on any map, it's impossible to learn it. There are some linguistic geniuses (in New York, in Buenos Aires, in Rome) who learned to read and write it, but cannot speak it; some can write it but not read what they write and others can read what they write but not understand what they are writing. It's one of those languages that change consonants and vowels constantly, often from one word to the next. A grammar never existed and would be unthinkable.

The first man who tried to write down the grammar of our language had to stop after a few months. He could not distinguish the first from the second person and the third from the second person plural. Singular and plural, passive, active, imperative, in our language, change with the mood of the speaker. Dative, accusative and imperative are used at any time, unexpectedly. There are no rules. We say what we like. We say, for instance: "He came to see whether to go or to come today or tomorrow" when we want to say: "He wants to know what's going on." And when we say: "It takes from everything something and from nothing everything as well to make anything," everyone but us gets confused and doesn't know what's going on. "Clear as the full moon in an empty glass" is one of our sayings, and "As long as a dog stretches himself he doesn't scratch himself" is another. It means approximately: "Even a blind man can hear what you see."

All this was not so funny when I came to think that making translations of English love stories would be much easier than shoveling snow at six schillings an hour and writing my private ideas on translation at home. After an eight-hour shift I earned enough to pay for a good meal in town. There was plenty of snow that winter. I even began to like the work. It's not too hard, it's good for the body, and the mind is free to wander on anything else. Snow, alas, is a hazardous occupation. From one day to the next, within a few hours, everything on which my life depended could be washed away by the rain.

72 73 10 9 8 7 6 5 4 3 2 1